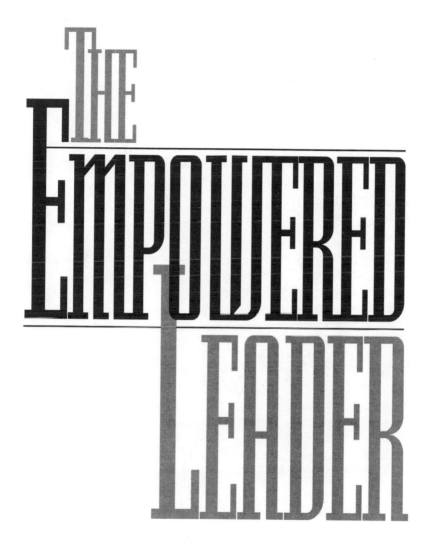

THE EMPOWERED LEADER

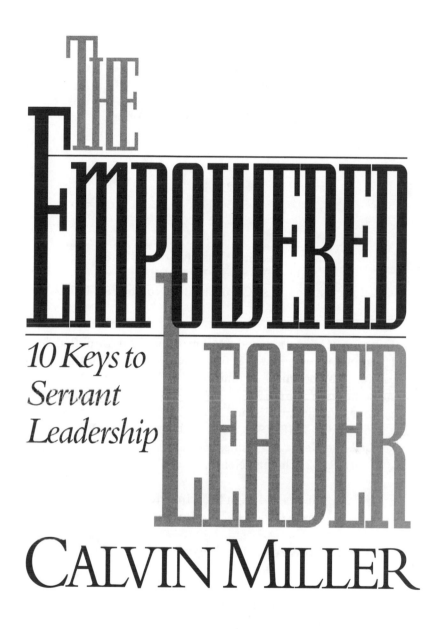

THE EMPOWERED LEADER

10 Keys to Servant Leadership

CALVIN MILLER

BROADMAN
& HOLMAN
PUBLISHERS

Nashville, Tennessee

4211-45
0-8054-1145-3

Dewey Decimal Classification: 303.3
Subject Heading: LEADERSHIP
Library of Congress Card Catalog Number 94-12752

Scripture quotations marked AMP are from The Amplified Bible,
Old Testament copyright © 1962, 1964 by Zondervan Publishing
House, used by permission, and the New Testament © The Lock-
man Foundation 1954, 1958, 1987, used by permission; KJV, the
King James Version; NIV, the Holy Bible, New International Version, copyright © 1973, 1978, 1984 by International Bible Society;
and NKJV, the New King James Version, copyright © 1979, 1980,
1982, Thomas Nelson, Inc., Publishers.

Interior design by Trina Hollister
Cover design by The Puckett Group

Library of Congress Cataloging-in-Publication Data

Miller, Calvin.
    The empowered leader: 10 keys to servant leadership / by
    Calvin Miller.
        p.   cm.
    Includes bibliographical references.
    ISBN 0-8054-1145-3
    1. Christian leadership.   I. Title.
BV652.1.M534   1995
253—dc20   94-12752
                                                  CIP

Table of Contents

Acknowledgments

I must offer my heartfelt thanks to two people. First of all, I am grateful to you, son Timothy, for being so everlastingly patient with me as I have tried to learn the world of computer graphics. Second, to you, Todd Holt, my faithful student assistant and reader, I will ever be grateful. I know your studies were demanding and yet you always seemed to find time for this manuscript.

Introduction

This book is not about success; it is about leadership. Robert A. Raines has reminded us in his dynamic title that *Success Is a Moving Target*. But leadership is a fixed goal at which we may take aim, fire, and gather in the trophy. God has never called anyone in ministry to be successful. But the whole of biblical and Christian history is a cumulative account of God's call to leadership.

Leadership is the compass of living. No other subject has been so explored in our day. Corporate heads and management specialists are constantly addressing the issue. They usually do this in an attempt to tell others how to ride the crest of corporate or political control. How should we who are Christians view leadership? How should our understanding of leadership differ from that of the secular "get-aheader"?

Every Christian who desires to become a leader must first know how to follow. While the major precepts of this book are drawn from a study of David of Israel, I suspect you bought this book because you are interested in developing your own leadership skills. It is my hope that this book serves both ends. For only when leadership is consistent with the biblical model can it really be servant leadership.

But is it consistent to talk about servant leadership in a book entitled *The Empowered Leader?* Let us grapple with this question as we seek to understand the relationship between power and servanthood.

I struggled in writing this book with issues of title and theme. Power is often a corrupting force in the secular world. Power is often a megaword in the megachurch. But King David called himself the *servant* of God. He hungered to be a person of obedience. Still he knew if he ever forged Israel into a nation, he must also be a man of power. Most of us who follow Christ prefer to follow servant-leaders rather than power-hungry tyrants. Is there a connection between empowered leadership and servant leadership?

At the outset, let me remind you of an important New Testament principle: If you would be king of all, you must become the servant of all (Matt. 20:27). A contemporary spin on this might be Zig Ziglar's belief that you can best achieve what you want in life if you are servant enough to help others achieve what they want in life.

A young deacon in a church I once served paid me the highest compliment when he said, "From your life I have learned that leadership is servanthood." I pray his words are true, for all who are going to be effective Christian leaders must first know how to follow Christ. Jesus warned all would-be entrepreneurs that it does little good to gain the whole world if we lose our souls (Luke 9:25). Christ was meek (Matt. 11:29), but He was no weakling. In all relationships, He must be seen as a man of empowered leadership. He did not quail before Herod nor simper before Pilate.

Jesus was a man whose servant-leadership powerfully declared itself. As a servant, He had submitted His life to God. In a similar way, we set free the real power of God's leadership in our lives by surrendering our weakness to His power.

At times in the lives of individuals, corporations, nations, and churches, there is a vacuum in the kind of leadership David's life defined. His meteoric rise in Israel came at a time when the nation floundered. It needed direction and vision. But herein lies the glorious paradox that inhabits the heart of Christian leadership: *only those who can obey are worthy to mandate*. David was worthy to lead people only because he had learned how to follow God.

If God has called you to Christian leadership, may this study challenge you to follow Christ to lead His people, His way. Only then can you become all that God has called you to be. Be firm in this intention. If God has called you to lead, do so! All leadership is strong. Weak leadership is no leadership. Out of spiritual meekness, boldly command.

Lead with power or do not call yourself a leader. But beware your strong pronouncements. Never assume a bogus authority that makes you feel you have the right to run things. Rather, bow your head and let God confer upon you the authority from above that will make you strong for the kind of leadership He requires.

In this book as we examine the various facets of David's leadership we will see him as a great yet ordinary man. "Great and ordinary" is the usual recipe of leadership. Most great leaders are wonderfully blind to their own significance. They are not ego-oriented, they are task-oriented. They never define themselves out of what they see in the mirror of corporate success. Rather they see themselves in the light of what God has called them to do. David was such a man. As you begin this study, it would be well for you to read 1 Samuel 16 through 2 Samuel 9. The progression of this study will be better understood if you are somewhat familiar with this period of David's life. As you read this book remember this: leadership is expected of leaders; indeed it is demanded. It is imperative for all who want to steer their church on a visionary course.

The chief points of this study offer a well-tried application for church leaders. But the principles may also apply to all who are engaged in corporate leadership as well. The Bible is relevant to every age. Make no mistake: the principles of leadership found in Scripture are applicable in every area of secular business. The Bible has sometimes been ignored by the Forbes-Magazine-Wall-Street-Journal person as a spiritual but pre-modern point of view. It is therefore often seen as beside the point in the right-now world of commerce, entrepreneurship, and technology. If such a notion permeates your view of how great leadership is to be done, let us reason together toward a more biblical viewpoint.

The objectives of this study are three. First, I want the wisdom of Scripture to speak a clear and usable word to every contemporary Christian leader. Second, I want those sound leadership themes that dominate current thinking to be linked with scriptural insight. I have tried to study contemporary management and to familiarize myself with the works of Harry Levinson, Peter Drucker, James MacGregor Burns, Thomas J. Peters, Warren Bennis, Burt Nanus, J. Paul Getty, Anthony Robbins, Philip Greenslade, Robert D. Dale, Kenneth Blanchard, Robert A. Raines, Bert Decker, Joe D. Batten, Max DePree, and others. You will find these pages dotted with sprinklings of their wisdom. I have sought to learn all I can from those secular and corporate thinkers I was not exposed to in my theological training. While this book is hardly exhaustive, I hope that I have presented those important principles that can make a difference in your leadership.

Finally, I hope to define Christian leadership in such a way that it escapes the haphazard reputation it often acquires. If this book furnishes you with new tools for leading, or a few fresh insights for service, I will be more than compensated.

Fostering an Honest
Servant Image

No human being can exist for long
without some sense of his own significance.
Whether he gets it by
shooting a haphazard victim on the street,
or by constructive work, or by rebellion,
or by psychotic demands in a hospital,
or by Walter Mitty fantasies,
he must be able to feel this I-count-for-something
and be able to live out that felt significance.

Rollo May,
Power and Innocence

The loss of the leader in some sense or other, the birth of misgiv-
ings about him, brings on the outbreak of panic.

Sigmund Freud,
Group Psychology and the Analysis of the Ego

Why man, he doth bestride the world like a colossus.

William Shakespeare,
Julius Caesar

Letter 1

Dear Leader:

Nobody's perfect! I understand that, OK? Still, I will only follow you if you convince me that you are more interested in being my leader than my boss. Bosses have a way of being too interested in their own career or in the corporate agenda. Believe me, I ought to know. I've had lots of bosses. They were all concerned only about my performance or my output. But to be honest, none of them seemed all that interested in me.

Now, don't tell me that I have nothing to worry about because this is a Christian organization. I've been a part of several churches that talked about leadership but practiced bosshood. They formed programs and built structures that prized people's worth on how much those people produced. Nursery duty, ushering, teaching Sunday School, driving the church van, giving or counting money—all these items became the measurement of worth. Tell me this: How is it that pastors who started out as leaders at last became only bosses, tending their religious machines, ordering them to produce growth?

I'm looking for a pastor who really believes that he who is greatest among you must be your servant (see Matt. 20:26). For me, Jesus abandoned His need for CEO status the night He knelt with a basin and towel and started washing feet. This is a modern age and all that, but I'm not looking for a pastor with an eelskin briefcase and matching Day-timer. I am far more eager to follow that leader who is unashamed to carry a basin and towel. That's the person who can lead as Jesus led, because that's the person who lives as Jesus lived. So, Pastor, get yourself a basin and towel and start serving. Then lead. I promise I'll be right behind you.

—Your Follower

1 Samuel 16:1–13; 18:1–8

It has been well said that "others are the mirrors to ourselves." To be an effective leader, you must be perceived as a leader by those you lead. So this study of leadership properly begins with a look at yourself. In chapters 16 and 18 of 1 Samuel, how others perceived David is laid out for your examination. In this chapter we will examine how others perceive your leadership. But keep these important qualities in the front of your mind as you move to the next chapter, where we shall consider how you perceive yourself.

The importance given to the self in the current "me" generation has sometimes displaced the importance of others. In an age where selfishness abounds, we must ask, "Does anybody really see a leader? In truth, does anybody see anybody?" Mike Mason says that in our day there is an overwhelming tendency to treat others as though they are merely extensions of ourselves. Compared with us, therefore, others do not seem to be quite real. "We see them as if through a haze, the haze of our own all-engulfing selfhood."[1] While Mason's rhetoric is firm, it is not altogether true. However high your own self-esteem rises, you do see other people. You observe them and measure all that they are against all that you are. Through such comparison you learn to define who you are as you take your place in this world. In this gawking society we must all live under the eye of others and leaders are scrutinized most of all.

How do leaders appear? In many ways. One thing, however, must be said of all of them: they appear to be leaders! Leadership always declares itself! Leadership never translates as anything less than what it is.

I have always disagreed with a poster that appeared in a Minneapolis barber shop. It presented a picture of Albert Einstein in a last, dramatic photograph. The great mathematical genius appears godlike in that photograph with his shock of wild, white hair flying over his keen, deep-set eyes. Yet the caption beneath the poster slurred, "A bad haircut can make anybody look dumb." The comment is both belittling and untrue. Einstein was a genius and can be perceived in no other way; the poster has lied.

Friedrich Nietzsche wrote that what most people want as a model for leadership is "a strong kind of man, most highly gifted in intellect and will."[2] The gifts that such men possess project as charisma. You may never have taken the time to define charisma, but you know it when you see it. Charisma, however, may be the least obvious to those who are closest to it. Why is it that in 1 Samuel, Jesse (and indeed, his other sons) seemed to be the last to see David as a potential candidate to be anointed king? Could it be that David's newness to Samuel caused his charisma to be so much more apparent than it was to the rest of his family? Had Jesse's family seen David so often that they had really ceased to see him at all?

David was, of course, not the only person in Scripture to whom this happened. Jesus Himself seemed to surprise the good people of His hometown by becoming quite popular. His great charisma as a leader was recognized everywhere, but mostly by those who did not know Him as well as the hometown folks did. They, in a sense, "overknew" Jesus.

There was a very ordinary boy in my hometown who seemed destined to amount to very little. But he surprised us all by becoming a nuclear physicist—a true leader in his field. Leaders survive in spite of our vain attempts to contain them within the overly familiar ways we know them. We see them too close-up. We cannot give them that separating perspective that they need to allow them a place in the larger world. We perceive them as little because our world is little, our view is little. Only as we allow them to outgrow our small perception can we see their leadership as large.

Why is this? John White suggests that leaders have a kind of elitism that cannot be denied. What is this elitism? A winning magnetism! The quality of this magnetism is most attractive in the leader who is not cocky or oversold on his or her charisma. Such a leader is psychologically secure with no need to toot his own horn. Even though it may be difficult for small minds to see, great leadership always proclaims itself.

We all grant Jesus His singular Godhead. Thus we cannot lump Him together with mere earthly leaders. But I wonder if this self-proclamation is what Jesus addressed when He said to His critics on Palm Sunday, "If these should hold their peace, the stones would immediately cry out" (Luke 19:40, KJV). Make no mistake about it! Who you are and what you are have a way of becoming known in the world.

Consider this question: If this self-proclaiming elitism characterizes your life, will not your devotion to God cause others to see the quality of your leadership? There is but one mix for great leadership that is unstoppable! Inward substance and outward daring—the Spirit of God and magnetic motivation all in a single life—is God's recipe for greatness.

What elusive qualities attend such secure persons? Could a primary quality be meekness? It is the meek who will inherit the earth (Matt. 5:5). The word *meek* is best translated "power under control." Jesus was called meek, not weak. Meekness is not a lack of power but the confidence that issues from it. W. E. Vine reminds us that our Lord was meek precisely because He had all the power of heaven at His command. At the cross ten thousand angels waited upon the one simple command Jesus never gave. God's Son was meek (Matt. 11:29), made so by His willingness to yield the use of His vast power to His Father's caprice. The meek weep and pray in secret, but in public they may defy heaven and earth. The meek inherit the very earth, said Jesus, because they never lose charge of their self-control. They only tremble before the possibility of becoming abusive with the power they know is theirs. They prefer to die rather than kill. They are like a shepherd defending his sheep or a mother protecting her young. They sacrifice without grumbling, give without calculating,

THE THREE INGREDIENTS

OF

GOD'S RECIPE FOR GREATNESS

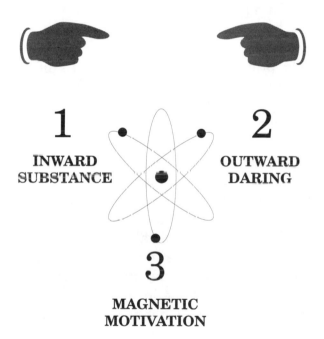

suffer without groaning.[3] Christ's true leaders are really His followers who use the levers of God and fulcrums of their esecure selfhood to move the world.

So in 1 Samuel 16–18, the embryonic charisma of the timid would-be leader of God surfaced as power. Samuel saw such charisma in a shepherd and poured the horn of oil on the boy's head. And what an old prophet immediately perceived as the marks of a leader, Israel would soon see and long celebrate.

The Perception of a Leader

In 1 Samuel 16:1–5, the prophet Samuel gathers Jesse's sons to look for a potential king. We cannot tell exactly who the prophet had in mind as he searched for a monarch in that dusty, one-camel town, Bethlehem. But we can be sure that the old prophet would see no one as fit for a king whom God did not approve as kingly. Again, all leaders must be self-proclaiming. Among Jesse's sons there were none whose demeanor said, "I would make a great king." This seems self-contradictory, for there were many of his sons whose appearance seemed to say that. They were kingly in stature, but not in demeanor. It is easy to be as tall as a king, but not easy to be as regal.

But how are we to gain the proper perception of great leadership? How can we look at all leaders through the bifocals of discernment? This implies that leadership must be seen two ways. Through the upper and weaker lens, we see appearance. Through the lower and stronger lens, we see demeanor. Leadership is not as it appears but as it performs.

Leadership is fibrous and tough, not easily torn by discouragement. It is very fluid, filtering through the lifestyles of the led. In short, leadership possesses leaders; leaders do not possess leadership. According to Max DePree, this ability to make courageous decisions in relationships is one of the key elements of leadership. "Followers expect a leader to face up to tough decisions. When conflict must be resolved, when justice must be defined and carried out, when promises need to be kept, when the organization needs to hear who counts—these are the times when leaders act with ruthless honesty and live up to their covenant with the people they lead."[4]

Yes, leadership owns leaders. It is not to be gained by studying books like this. It is innate. It seems to be encoded in the DNA. It bonds to the very souls of those it possesses. It may be called forth by crisis, but it is never produced by crisis. Did German aggression produce Winston Churchill? No, it but released him. The inhumane and greedy advance of the Third Reich produced an inner fury that unbound Churchill's virility. It called a nation to survival. Since books cannot make leaders, this one exists more to waken and define your capabilities in leadership than to create them.

Avoiding Superficiality

The old prophet's search for a king in 1 Samuel 16:1–13 had been conditioned with inner vision. Long before he anointed David, Samuel had anointed Saul as king (1 Sam. 10:23–24). Samuel had found Saul, a king who looked good in the upper lens of his bifocals. Tall, debonair, handsome, Harvard-Business-School Saul. So impressive was Saul physically that Samuel mistook appearance for ability. He raised his horn of oil and anointed only a superstar, not a leader. The bifocals of his search had caused him to look superficially for a national leader. With the weaker upper lens he had been bedazzled by Saul's regal appearance. Unfortunately Saul's appearance was all there was that was regal about him. So Samuel opted for image over substance, and Saul became king.

Although Saul was not a good king, he was a necessary king. He was necessary because he became the ultimate picture of how kings should *not* be and how they should *not* rule. Saul was, as I have said, superficial. But how is superficiality to be defined? Superficial comes from two Latin words, *super* and *facia,* which mean "upon the face" or "face value." We are superficial when what we appear to be is all there is to us. When what others see in us is all they get in us, we are not so much transparent as superficial.

This is what Stephen Covey refers to as following the personality ethics of the corporate world. He calls it "symbol without substance. It is the 'get rich quick' scheme promising 'wealth without work.' And it might even appear to succeed—but the schemer remains."[5] Great leadership is that which, when touched, quickly tells us it is too deep to be touched. Below the apparent surface of great leadership are deep souls whose understanding threatens to swallow us. Yet, the more we probe great leaders, the more we become aware that their insights are bottomless—their wisdom is too vast to outline or format. David was such a leader. He was much more than he appeared to be. Saul, by contrast, was only what he appeared to be—no more, no less.

Damien, the missionary to the lepers of Hawaii, was a paradigm of servant leadership. As we will affirm throughout this book, the real power of leadership lies in servanthood. Damien, of Molokai, had no resources to speak of, yet he appeared rich. He committed himself to the malformed and dying. In those he served, he wakened an ability to transcend themselves. His selflessness caused the hopeless to care less about their own suffering than they did about the needs of others. Damien gave such dignity to the dying that he brought the word hope back to their vocabulary. He proved that servant leadership is never a saucer where surface and depth lie close together. Leadership is rather a well where the substance of the soul lies deep and its well rope is long to reach the cold, pure depths.

What denotes servant leadership? A strange unawareness of ego. Servant leaders are task-centered. Because they tend to pick great tasks, they always feel overwhelmed and inadequate. Because they feel inadequate, they seek to look beyond themselves for answers. They don't do this to be heroic. They do it to be honest. They know they don't have all the answers.

Their commitment to the task means that real leaders hire to their weakness. They do this consistently even when the strengths of those they hire further illuminate their own weaknesses. They know that the hiring of strong associates helps them eliminate the weaknesses in their organization. Strong organizations are more important to them than egoistic reputations. They crave a strong organization above a good image. They deplore incompetency, even when incompetents by contrast point up their strengths. Their feeling of weakness has a wonderful spiritual dimension. Feelings of inadequacy in Christian leaders cause them to compensate for their weaknesses by turning inwardly to Christ.

A Universal Pecking Order

We often arrive at leader selection by imitating the action of the prophet (1 Sam. 16). Samuel went to Bethlehem to look for a king. Jesse of Bethlehem presented Samuel an all-star line-up of sons. Jesse's sons appeared to be rugged, CEO types. But in the process of sorting through their appearance, Samuel felt a need to read their résumés very closely.

How unlike Samuel we are when we choose. All too often we line up our supposed staff, eyeball their credentials, and vote them in or out on their appearance alone. The mistake of Jesse is a universal fault. He calls Samuel in to begin his search with Abinadab. Jesse's most impressive son seems the place to begin. But the Bible holds a vital lesson of leadership. Each time we play this image roulette we opt for leadership by relativism. Relativism is the way we compare résumés to arrive at the most ideal. Every company or church has its pecking order. But leadership is *not* a matter of comparing the best virtues of all the assembled candidates. The old prophet discovers a faulty system. The right candidate is not present—the contest is not inclusive enough. God's chosen leader is rarely in the line-up. David is out tending sheep. It is his absence, not his presence, that proclaims itself.

It's always that way. We're not altogether sure when leadership is present, but we are always sure when it is absent. My favorite Arthur myth reminds me that when England needed a king, there was a sword in a stone. *Excalibur* was the magic word that belonged to the spiritual leadership in that day. We too often ballot our choices for leaders, picking and choosing in our relativistic way. But history repeatedly teaches us that running through a stack of résumés is often a faulty way to look for leadership. Only the real king can wrest the sword from the stone. The holder of the title *leader* often comes from the shadows of obscurity. On such unsuspected persons the mantle falls.

Ability vs. Sociability

But doesn't 1 Samuel 16:11 clearly show that leaders are often recluses? Are they not slow social mixers? Yes, all too often leaders are loners. Lincoln, it is said, walked at midnight and in his loneliness grieved American division and plotted reunion. We can see in the life of Jesus that Gethsemane was more than the garden of his passion. It was a daily principle. Jesus Himself withdrew because only as He created aloneness did His life among people have any content. Must it always be this way? I think so. A friend of mine once said that you cannot help people if you're always with people. Obsessive glad handers rarely contribute much to the welfare of others. It is not altogether true, but those who have a fierce need to be the life of the party rarely ever lead.

I was touched in reading a biography of William Carey, the quiet saint who led the modern mission movement. Carey led as a suffering, lonely person. Perhaps one reason leaders are alone a lot is that they live so far out ahead of those they lead. They often have such a clear picture of where their constituency should be, they are eager to bring their followers to that place. So fierce is their need to move people rapidly toward their ideals that they often tend to get out ahead of their followers. Hence, the zeal of their leadership can, at times, isolate them from their followers.

The Beautiful People

The Scripture says David was "beautiful" (1 Sam. 16:12). If he was so uncomely that he did not appear in Jesse's line-up of sons, what are we to make of this word *beautiful?* David must have been one whose inner life rendered him beautiful. What is it that makes leaders beautiful? Isn't it selflessness, that never-never state of servanthood? Beautiful people are others-centered.

How much we have been influenced by the life of Mother Theresa of Calcutta. Malcolm Muggeridge called the life of Mother Theresa "Something Beautiful for God." Her life is beautiful because, while she exemplifies leadership, she does it with no hint of self-interest.

Beautiful then is often defined as being lost in a cause bigger than ourselves. Further, inner beauty is enhanced when our own glory is unimportant. In such cases we exist so much for the cause, we are unable to regard ourselves in a superior manner. Many who conquer great worlds are oddly haunted by feelings of inferiority. Newton's tomb in Westminster Abbey is characterized by one of his own quotes in which he likened himself to a child lost on the seashore of life, looking for a prettier pebble than the rest had been able to find.[6] What an understatement of his life, for if we blot out his life, the spectrum is gone and gravity is undefined.

Self-centeredness is ugly; altruism is beautiful. Stephen Covey says that self-centeredness is like Israel's Dead Sea, for it welcomes in freshness but grows stagnant because it will not give. Yet selfishness is a word commonly used to define our culture. Stagnation comes from the receiving life. Personal growth comes from the giving life.

The Spiritual Life of a Leader

The spiritual life of a leader gathers itself around a single powerful idea—servanthood. We will touch this theme often throughout this book but the authority for our view will be in four Greek words.

A *diakonos* is a worker; the word emphasizes the servant role in relationship to what he is asked to do. A *doulos* is a slave; the word emphasizes the servant's accountability to his master. A *huperetes* is a servant in relation to his superior; the *huperetes* always is under the authority of his superior. A *leitourgos* is a steward; this is my favorite of these words because it speaks of the servant in relation to the organization.[7]

The coming of the Spirit meant everything in David's life. Such visitation from God is never a single consultation but a process. God does not merely accompany great spiritual leaders. He inhabits them. It is a quality of spiritual leadership that He influences from the inside out.

It is the indwelling God who distinguishes religious leaders from secular leaders. No matter how wise a secular leader is, he or she rates second to the God-called leader. Is it not a wonderful thing to see ordinary human beings inhabited by a sense of holy call? We may see it in the virtue of William Gladstone, David Livingstone, Martin Luther King, and Jim Elliott. Do we not touch it in a William Carey, Gladys Aylward, or Joan of Arc?

The spiritual leader is one who yields to God for his or her best work. Such leaders have been with Jeremiah to the potter's house to watch an artistic God shape the clay (Jer. 18). Michaelangelo wrote of this shaping activity in terms of God as a Master Sculptor. The image is wonderful, for none of us knows who we really are; we are waiting for the sculptor to cut away all unnecessary stone from the block and reveal our true being unto ourselves.

> The best of artists has that thought alone
> Which is contained within the marble shell;
> The sculptor's hand can only break the spell
> To free the figures slumbering in the stone.[8]

The New Testament Words

That Form the Boundaries of

Servant Leadership

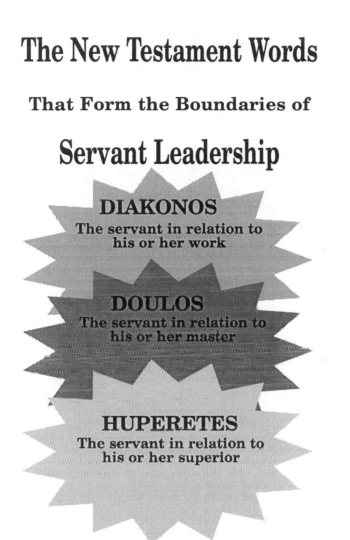

DIAKONOS
The servant in relation to
his or her work

DOULOS
The servant in relation to
his or her master

HUPERETES
The servant in relation to
his or her superior

It isn't just that this sculpturing Jehovah is revealing us to the world; He is revealing us to ourselves as well. Only God knows what our finished and glorified selves will look like. In 1 John 3:2 we are reminded that we are in the process of being formed in his usable likeness. We can't know in the moment how we will finally look. But we know that when He has finished with us, it will be wonderful.

God is ever creating leadership by removing our showy facade and revealing our true selves from out of the stone. Rene Dubos describes the imaginative care of Eskimo sculptors. "As the carver held the raw fragment of ivory in his hand, he turned it gently this way and that way, whispering to it, 'Who are you? Who hides in you?'" These carvers rarely set out to shape particular form.[9]

The question of these sculptors is not one God asks of us but it is one we must ask of ourselves. Who are we as leaders and what form will our final leadership profile take. It is the indwelling Spirit that fashions and shapes the emerging leader.

Why do we so admire those who seem to serve under the Spirit? Because He inhabits extraordinary people? No. Because those who might have used life for their own ends are brought under a more splendid sovereignty. Our admiration of such leaders is not because of their submission, for much plainer souls may do that. Their great appeal lies in the fact that they bring heaven and earth into synthesis. They are the needy who must marry weak acceptance and powerful decisiveness.

How Others Perceive Our Commitment

This synthesis of God and ordinary souls commands our attention, not because it is flashy but because it is rare. Great spiritual leaders do not stop us with their reputation, but with their devotion to His inescapable importance. Ever yearning for more of the force of Christ, they also long for more commitment. Paul called himself the "least of all saints" and the "chief of sinners" (1 Tim. 1:15). Feeling that they are achieving little, such demurring leaders turn the "world upside down" (Acts 17:6). They don't do this to be known as independent thinkers. They do it because they are servants or captives of Grace: Paul even called himself a slave or *doulos* of Christ (Phil. 1:1). He regarded his leadership as nothing more than a command performance. So it is with other great Christian leaders across the ages. They are unable to live without the Savior. He absorbs all their interest, dictates their need, and beckons them to His agenda.

As Christ is track one of great leadership, His agenda is track two. Servant leaders carry to completion what God has given them to do. They have, as Paul put it, a certain race to run: "Therefore, I do not run like a man running aimlessly. . . . No, I beat my body and make it my slave so that after I have preached to others, I myself will not be disqualified for the prize" (1 Cor. 9:26–27, NIV).

This was Paul's cry to be disciplined and orderly in his pursuit of Christ's objectives. His was a focused passion. Paul did not try to do everything. He narrowed his list of things to do. He kept his leadership agenda simple: "When I came to you, brothers, I did not come with eloquence or superior wisdom. . . . For I resolved to know nothing while I was with you except Jesus Christ and him crucified" (1 Cor. 2:1–2, NIV)

The singular devotion of men and women of God leaves their world with a singular perception of them. Empowered leadership is empowered servanthood. Paul wrote, "My message and my preaching were not with wise and persuasive words, but with a demonstration of the Spirit's power, so that your faith might not rest on men's wisdom, but on God's power" (1 Cor. 2:4–5, NIV).

Conclusion

The century about to dawn requires servant leadership. The church everywhere has come under a microscope because of her hypocrisy and corruption. She has really been under the scope of media scrutiny because many of her pastors and evangelists have lacked leadership and integrity. Thus the number one quality that must mark tomorrow's leaders is servanthood.

But this servanthood will have to couple with other far-ranging executive qualities as well. Frank Nunlist, of the Worthington Corporation, pictures the leader of the year 2000 as a young man with broad goals and great influence. This leader will specialize in harmonizing the conflicting interests of individuals and the corporation. "He will spend more time in creating satisfactions for people as individuals and will tend to destroy some of our present concepts of mass management."[10] But we cannot wait until the twenty-first century to begin building today's leaders. The future must be purchased in the present.

We cannot set a date out there when we will begin promoting servanthood as a leadership style. This kind of leadership is nurtured in the Spirit by following Jesus. Servant leaders generally are created not in commanding others but in obeying their Commander. In such a mystique, executive arrogance is not possible. The yielded leader is always an incarnation of Christ, the real leader of His church.

Seeing Yourself as a Leader: Learning the Art of Self-Perception

The best way to create a good, healthy self-image is to be honest about self-definition. I would like to sing, but I can't.

Steve Brown,
No More Mr. Nice Guy

[warty bliggens] considers himself to be
the center of the . . . universe
the earth exists to grow toadstools for him to sit under
the sun to give him light by day and the moon
and wheeling constellations
to make beautiful
the night for the sake of warty bliggens

Don Marquis,
"archy and mehitabel"

If we do not evaluate our own behavior, or having evaluated it, we do not act to improve our conduct where it is below our standards, we will not fulfill our need to be worthwhile and we will suffer as acutely as when we fail to love or be loved. Morals, standards, values, or right and wrong behavior are all intimately related to the fulfillment of our need for self-worth.

William Glasser,
Reality Therapy

Letter 2

Dear Leader:

I have a friend whose Uncle Jesse really knew how to play softball. With a good oak bat, he could knock a ball a country mile. He was the kind of batter you like to have in the circle with all the bases loaded. He continued playing ball well into his fifties, still batting like he did in his twenties.

But it was in his fifties that we began to see the startling first effects of Alzheimer's disease. Suddenly and without warning, in a big game, when the score was tight and the team was counting on Jesse to break the deadlock and win the game, his mind quit supporting the sport. When it was his turn, he went to bat just as he always had. He bent over and picked up a couple of handfuls of dirt to tighten his grip, just as he always did. He tapped the bat a couple of times on the fiberboard of homeplate. As usual, he scuffed his feet in the dirt backwards, pawing the earth like a rabid animal. He crouched with the bat slightly off his shoulder. Just like always he spit in the dirt, faced the pitcher and waited. The pitch came. It was in there. He knocked it a stem-winding. It was out of the park—a home run! Jesse threw the bat down and ran down the lefthand foul line to third base.

Third base!

It was a bad sign.

Things went downhill pretty fast after that. Uncle Jesse lost his mind faster than anybody I've ever known. Six months later he didn't know his wife when she brought him his breakfast. He didn't even know his own name. But one thing Jesse never forgot was how to hit a fast pitch. He could still belt the ball a country mile. He always knew enough to hit the ball and run. He just had no idea where to run or why he was running in the first place.

Softball's a hard game when you don't know who you are. So is life!

I've been part of this church for a long time. A couple of preachers back, we had a pastor who never seemed to find out who he was. He preached other people's sermons. He copied other people's programs almost entirely. There was this big church up in the windy city, and he felt like if he could duplicate it exactly, our church would be just as big. He even dressed like that preacher too.

All of us on the board kept peeling back the layers of his ego, trying to find out who he really was. We never could find out. I expect it was because he didn't know either. I never did watch him play softball, but I always wondered if he could hit the ball. Even when he connected, I wonder what base he ran to? Bet it was third.

—Your Follower

1 Samuel 17:19–54

As a leader, your work, like your life, must bear the scrutiny of your own tough evaluation. You will do God no favor if you charge out into the world with no real understanding of who you are. Ignorance about yourself is a self-imposed limitation that will keep your full leadership potential from developing. Did David understand who he was? Let's see how much he really knew about who he was and what God expected of him.

In the passage on which this chapter is focused, David seems to conquer the inner giant of self-doubt as he battles his formidable outer foe, Goliath. The toughness of such an outer foe, however, may be a piece of cake in comparison to our struggle against the inner foe. The reason many potential leaders never really develop has little to do with the toughness of their outer foes. Outer foes and tough circumstances are roughly the same for all. The giants on the inside are the real problems.

The giants we fight on the inside do battle with our self-image. The development of a winning self-perception has little to do with how we see ourselves in the moment. How we see ourselves finishing up in life is the key. One of the most significant questions Peter Drucker asks is this: "What do you want to be remembered for?" Such a question entails our final self-perception. Such a question does not ask, "How is the race going?" but "What about the finish line of life?"

Peter Drucker relates that when he was thirteen "an inspiring teacher of religion" asked his class of boys, "What do you want to be remembered for?" None of them knew how to reply. Then the teacher said, "I didn't expect you to be able to answer it. But if you still can't answer it by the time you're fifty, you will have wasted your life."[1] Getting a clear view of how we want to end up has everything to do with defeating the momentary giants of our lives.

Many psychologists believe that persons of low self-esteem are not only more frenzied in their lifestyles, they are also less imaginative than those with better self-acceptance. They are, therefore, far less likely to become successful leaders than those who have learned to manage the inner foe of self. David's competence did not come from a trumped up, latent egotism. His dependence was upon God.

Still, you must be careful as you balance self-denial and self-esteem in your life; you must not pretend that faith in God means automatic self-esteem. Robert Schuller has repeatedly pointed out that, as a group, evangelical Christians consistently rate lowest in self-esteem polls. Why? Perhaps because of certain post-Reformation explanations of human depravity. How about your own church experience? Were you ever taught as a child to see yourself as loathsome to your Maker? When we see ourselves as loathsome to God, we become more loathsome to ourselves. Jean-Paul Sartre in *The Flies* has a man crying out, "I stink! Oh, how I stink! I am a mass of rottenness. . . . I have sinned a thousand times . . . and I reek to heaven!"[2]

For four hundred years Protestants have been telling themselves that they are totally depraved. For forty decades we have put ourselves so far down that we find it hard to see the God-given good in our lives. We must never excuse our fallen condition. Human sinfulness is the reason for the cross of Christ. Even though we are fallen, however, we are also stamped with the *imago dei,* the image of God. We should legitimately celebrate the good things that are part of us. This is especially true of those who have made Christ Lord of their lives.

We often speak of the imperative of self-esteem. Certainly self-esteem is imperative in the life of secure leaders. But what is self-esteem? Stanley Coopersmith defines self-esteem as "the evaluation which the individual makes and customarily maintains with regard to himself: it expresses an attitude of approval or disapproval, and indicates the extent to which the individual believes himself to be capable, significant, successful, and worthy."[3] For the real leader, this self evaluation is not only important, it is essential. Max DePree agrees: "Followers adamantly demand that a leader possess a high degree of integrity when it comes to *self-perception*. A combination of self-confidence and humility seems to me to be crucial, for this oxymoronic quality makes it possible for the group to be decisive."[4]

Is it true that people of low self-esteem can manage but never lead? One thing is sure: leadership and management often fall into widely separate categories. I will comment more fully on this in key 8. For the moment let me distinguish between leadership and management by saying, no one is really eager to be managed, but the entire world is hungry to be led. Consider the powerful truth of these words: "If you want to manage somebody, manage yourself. Do that well and you'll be ready to stop managing. And start leading."[5]

Often managers only manage what leaders have brought into being. Mark this down: *this book is not a call to manage, but to lead.* In David we examine the life of a leader who found that the will of God was the only adequate mirror to his self-image. Once David found out what God wanted with him, the direction of his leadership was decided. It is not such a fearsome thing to lead once you see your leadership as a part of God's overall plan for His world.

This sense of a consistent plan is what the world would like to see in the church. Unfortunately they rarely find it. The church looks enfeebled and divided. Christians have taken the world's greatest reality and made it appear illusory. We have come to represent to our hungry world what Warren Bennis calls the "Age of Unreality." What does Bennis mean by this?

He means that we now justify our moral and faulty behavior in terms of what seems right to us. We then come to accept our moral incompetencies as insistent. Politicians and preachers alike seem to lie and commit adultery, steal, embezzle, and behave fraudulently. They go right on being supported by people who steal, embezzle, and behave fraudulently. "Rather than protesting all this doubletalk, the American people seem not only to accept it but to understand it. This, then, is the Age of Unreality."[6]

God is in charge of our world! It is high time that Christians quit worrying so much about their image and take hold of some great vision. Maybe, then, we can appear real in this age of unreality. God is sovereign, and all of history is but the train for which God laid the rails in eternity past.

When I was a boy, I was fascinated by the railroad tracks that passed my home. My mother told me there were engineers who drove trains more than four hundred miles in a single day.

"It must be hard to drive trains such long distances," I said to her.

"No" she countered. "Engineers only pull levers; the journey is up to the rails." I'm sure she oversimplified the task of the engineers, but she did put my mind at rest. Great Christian leaders ride the rails of divine obedience. They are responsible for levers. They are responsible for the distance. But they are not responsible for the direction. Direction is God's compass, given to those who lead.

David, like all great people, had set the throttle of life's engine to serve the pleasure of God. Those rails carried him to the very pinnacle of history. Should we not, therefore, seek only those rails that are labeled "the pleasure of God"? Should we not always pray that we will stay on track? Then only will we keep in touch with meaning. Meaning and failure never keep company in life. Neither do low self-esteem and pleasing God. Seeing and accepting your God-given strengths will make you usable to the God who gave you those strengths.

The Hard Work of Self-Analysis

Self-analysis is hard work! It is tiring work! It is endless work! But worse than all these things, it holds an implicit danger. It can be futile work. Self-analysis can become so self-absorbing that it keeps us from turning outward to see what we really should be doing. It is dangerously interiorating. When we are working overtime to understand ourselves we are usually letting a lot of other things go. It is a kind of *paralysis diabolicus!* Satan likes us best when we are completely absorbed in trying to figure ourselves out, because at such moments all forward motion in our lives stops.

Those persons and churches who accomplish a great deal are not persons or churches who necessarily understand themselves better than small achievers. They are merely those who are unconcerned about self-analysis. In many cases, they don't consider themselves important. Paul, near the end of his life, summed up his selflessness when he said: "But whatever was to my profit I now consider loss for the sake of Christ. What is more, I consider everything a loss compared to the surpassing greatness of knowing Christ Jesus my Lord, for whose sake I have lost all things. I consider them rubbish, that I may gain Christ" (Phil. 3:7–8, NIV). There is often a thin line between too much self-analysis and a healthy self-awareness.

The only real way to find out who we are is through relationships. In the ego-feedback we receive from others, we make the necessary adjustments to our lives. For instance, when someone says, "You preached too long, Pastor," I consider their feedback important. For the sake of bettering my preaching style, I must find out if this criticism is true and, if so, I must adjust.

"You looked foolish tonight in moderating the committee meeting," or "Don't you think you spend too much time on the tennis courts?" or "Are you spending enough time in the study?" Such questions as these come either from sincere concern or critical spirits. But empowered leaders process them through the filter of personal sensitivity to determine their source and properly evaluate them. Nonetheless, once processed, such statements must be implemented or discarded, and life must move on.

David, in 1 Samuel 17:26, was a person in touch with both his limitations and the unlimited power of God. He turned outward to consider the crisis, not thinking of all his personal weaknesses. No paralysis intimidated David! What was to be done? David was not sure! One thing was sure: wringing his hands would not help.

Then come questions from a foe that David must first process and then reply to: "Who is this uncircumcised Philistine that he should defy the armies of the living God?" (1 Sam. 17:26, NIV). David must first answer Goliath's question, not so Goliath will know who David is, but so that David himself will know who David is. Without knowing who he is, David cannot assess his strengths and weakness and be reminded of his need to depend on God. Here is a giant who requires not David's understanding but God's rebuke.

Now David, a fledgling teenager, gives himself to a concrete action in a cause bigger than David's need to know who he is. Now he may pick up those five smooth stones and give God his all in service. David's action had nothing to do with the psychological lie that says self-understanding above all. The world is not generally helped along by people who are driven to understand themselves but by people who want to change their world.

There is an abundance of neuroses in most world-changers. But would they have been world-changers if they had spent more time preoccupied with their hang-ups? I doubt it. Make no mistake about it! We should never champion neurotics in leadership. But I am convinced that great leaders are rarely normal, well-adjusted people. Frankly, which of us is not a bit tired of normalcy anyway? Give us rather those dream-driven people whose affection for what they want to accomplish sometimes leaves them lopsided. If they lead effectively and accomplish good dreams for their world, can we not forgive them for paying so little attention to themselves?

Getting God Involved in Self-Study

Let us move from Goliath's fight with David to the issue of self-study. Before Goliath's challenge, David's own family caused him to doubt himself. In 1 Samuel 17:28, was David immobilized by Eliab's criticism that he was more a shepherd than a soldier? Such criticisms usually are not effective in building a good self-image. It is usually true that negative criticisms hurt us. But isn't it also true that those negative criticisms, in the long run, are the ones that reshape our souls? Still, when we are swamped with too much incoming negative feedback, we are usually smothered in depression. Bowled over by self-doubt, we are then unable to use the incoming data to improve our weaknesses.

There are two items that we should always include in our self-study. The first is that relational feedback we get from those we serve. Power leaders are usually power listeners. Listening to those who criticize our position is important for spiritual growth and advancement. Jim Lundry capitalizes on this idea: "It has been said that feedback is the breakfast of champions. Although this saying has broad implications, it certainly is true that champion communicators make sure they understand what the other person is saying."[7]

Empowered leaders use all incoming comments to shape their leadership. Power listening is the way to become a power communicator, and power communication is the route of power leadership. We must listen to know who we are.

The second and most important aspect of empowered leadership has to do with getting God involved in our self-study. How do we discover those spiritual forces that give maximum clout to our leadership? First, we make sure that we are a people of the disciplines—prayer, Bible study, and ministry. By prayer, I include both speaking and listening. By Bible study, I mean personal, devotional Bible study, not merely sermon preparation time.

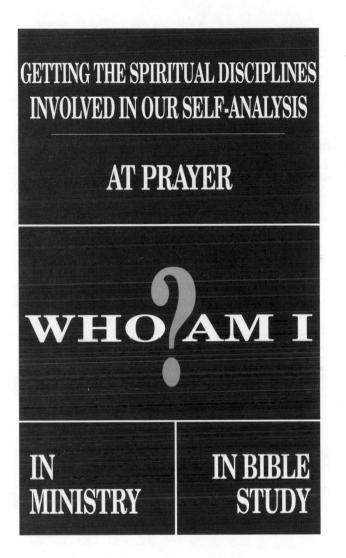

GETTING THE SPIRITUAL DISCIPLINES INVOLVED IN OUR SELF-ANALYSIS

AT PRAYER

WHO AM I?

IN MINISTRY

IN BIBLE STUDY

Ministry to others may be the most important of the disciplines. Personal ministry is not a cure-all for discovering the heart of God, but administrating the church without it leads to a spiritual sterility that blinds our hearts to who we are. As we have already said, empowered leaders have God's power conferred upon them. They never seize power to wield it in their own name. But how do they call this power forth spontaneously from their souls? It is summoned as God is invited to be the center of all His plans for His church.

Such conferred power, therefore, proceeds from our union with Christ. Jesus gives us the power of leadership as we offer Him our weakness. Our self-study then becomes self-sacrifice. We lay our lives on the altar and the altar infuses our dying with His life. In our willingness to die with Christ, His power is conferred (Gal. 2:20).

The Three Tenses of Success:
Letting Your Past Guide Your Future
While Your Future Instructs the Present

The future you is always beckoning to the present you and saying, "Come on, get with it." We see ourselves in the future as highly successful. In fact, what we want to become usually jaundices our present sense of discipline by creating future images of success, wealth, and power. Steven Covey's "funeral exercise" (of trying to get us to see ourselves at our own funeral) for most would-be CEO's is a grandiose picture of utter wealth.

This all reminds me a bit of the dying superachiever who asked to be buried in his solid gold Cadillac, propped up behind the steering wheel, with a five-dollar cigar in his hand. After his last gasp, the funeral director honored his request. As he was lowered, in his car, into his overlarge grave, a bystander was heard to remark, "Man, that is really living."

Jesus had a similar story about a man whose definition of success was building bigger and bigger barns. It was easy for others to see his final success, but for him it was a disinheritance. Jesus' definition of success would allow for no self-serving images. Our final self-image must be an image of servanthood. How can our future guide our present leadership? It ought to be easy to tell how you are going to lead by looking at how you have lead in the past. Looking back, like looking forward, can inform us. It can also trip us up. So often in looking back, we stumble over the future. *Always analyze the past in preparing for the future* was one of the leadership principles of Attila the Hun, according to Wess Roberts.[8]

THE TENSES OF
LEADERSHIP

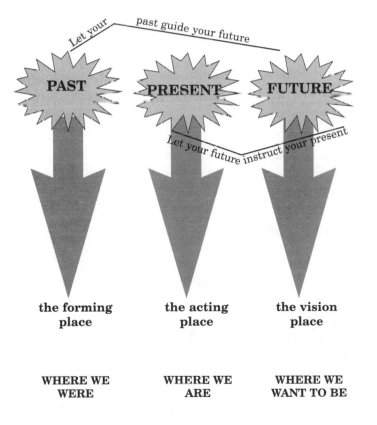

| the forming place | the acting place | the vision place |

| WHERE WE WERE | WHERE WE ARE | WHERE WE WANT TO BE |

It is in looking back that we are tempted to cherish our heritage while growing blind to our destiny. Nevertheless, our past performance can also instruct us. If we have done poorly, our past, painfully examined, can help us toward a better future. If we have repeatedly done something well in the past, we have established a pattern of hope. David, in 1 Samuel 17:34–36, remembered how well he had done with a slingshot in the past. So he proposed to transfer training. What worked with a bear would probably work with a giant, he reasoned. His slingshot methodology was transferable. Empowered leadership wisely makes the past its teacher. Goliath fell prey to a proven principle. Empowered leadership takes good notes on life and writes all its future lectures out of past examinations.

Power Leadership and Traditional Thinking

Tradition walks looking backwards. It has for a major flaw its ability to keep us from seeing all the wondrous possibilities of the moment. Why is this a sin? Because "a mind open to our world's unlimited possibilities is free to see comparisons in everyday things that can lead to revolutionary advancements. Sir Isaac Newton's first hint that led to his important discovery of the spectrum came when, in watching a child's soap bubble, he noted the changes of the image that appeared on its rounded surface."[9] Would Newton have seen the rainbows in the bubbles if he had been content reading the past?

The past may either be a great teacher or a cumbersome pitfall. The past for most church leaders is not a lectern of hope and progress but a ball and chain that fastens all future technique to the way we used to do it. Tradition teaches us to cherish good values, but it also leaves us in yesterday—trapped helpless before the ever-changing onslaught of movements and trends.

Traditionalists rarely carry watches. They only read diaries. They don't care what time it is—only what time it *was.* To be fully aware of the present time too much obligates them to live in the risky now. To these traditionalists, the most dreaded and threatening sound is the roaring tick-tock of all those infernal clocks, whose pendulums, never stopping, spoil their comfort. What might really work in church programs slides quietly toward the rear of opportunity. While trying to hold on to what used to work, we find those less afraid of pendulums far outdistancing us. Southern Baptists, who did so much at mid-century to teach innovation to American evangelicalism, should reexamine this truth. Yesterday's innovators easily become today's traditionalists.

But more important than this is the truth that yesterday's exciting innovations are the boring drudgeries of today. Boredom comes from repetition, drudgery from meaninglessness. Drudgery and boredom together are a double threat. Peter Drucker comments: "Most work is doing the same thing again and again. The excitement is not the job—it is the result. Nose to the grindstone, eyes on the hills. If you allow a job to bore you, you have stopped working for results. Your eyes, as well as your nose, are then on the grindstone."[10]

There is probably only one way to end boredom of long standing. It begins by admitting you are in the wrong place. I so often have other preachers ask me, "How do I know when it is time to change churches?" The answer for preachers is the same as for all other leaders. Again Drucker offers us his splendid counsel: "The right decision is to quit if you are in the wrong place, if it is basically corrupt, or if your performance is not being recognized. Promotion itself is not the important thing. What is important is to be eligible, to be equally considered. If you are not in such a situation, you will all too soon begin to accept a second-rate opinion of yourself. Sometimes a change—a big change or a small change—is essential in order to stimulate yourself again."[11] The key issue is to remember that tradition festers boredom and boredom inhibits creativity. David's story illustrates how innovation may deliver us of giants. But take stock of your hang-ups! Many are more afraid of abandoning tradition than they are of fighting giants.

David, in 1 Samuel 17:38–39, was urged to wear armor to fight the giant. No doubt that day he was told that "his sling-shot innovations" were not time-tested nor battle-approved. He did try on Saul's armor, but decided that if he was going to fight giants, he would do it in his own non-traditional way. David's self-understanding was thorough. He knew himself—what worked for him and what did not. There may have been thousands of other soldiers for whom giant-fighting was a matter of armor and sword. Still, David's own self-perception taught him that slingshots were right for him.

To know who we are and how we best fight giants makes winning possible. More than that, knowing who we are is the foundation of secure and innovative leadership.

But whatever leadership is, it is not a hankering after success. Leadership lies in a hunger to understand and make the world better. It is fueled by learning. Leaders are students. They are never narrowly-students but students whose studies are varied and wide.

J. Paul Getty, himself an Oxford Scholar, said that most of those who really succeed are liberal arts scholars and not narrowly trained technicians. Technical experts may serve in middle management, but a broad education more fully prepares the young executive for top leadership.[12] I believe Getty's principles should be firmly applied to pastoral leadership. The pastor who knows only the Bible may possess only authority without understanding. The pastor who knows art, literature, sports, novels, movies, and the newspaper will bring imagination and freshness to both his leadership and his pulpit. The best pastor-leaders are those who can integrate knowledge from many different fields and apply it specifically and biblically to the Christian life.

THE EFFECTIVE INTEGRATED LEARNER

Experience • Art and Hobbies • Education •
Worship • Religious Worldview • Professional
Networks • Experience • Art and Hobbies •
Education • Worship • Religious Worldview •
Professional Networks • Experience • Art and
Hobbies • Education • Worship • Religious
Worldview • Professional Networks •
Experience • Education •
Worship • Professional
Netwo bbies •
Educati dview •
Pr and
Hobb igious
Worl ks •
E
Wor sional
Net
Educ
Profess Art and
Hobbi ligious
Worldview etworks •
Experience Education •
Worship • Relig w • Professional
Networks • Experience • Art and Hobbies •
Education • Worship • Religious Worldview •
Professional Networks • Experience • Art and
Hobbies • Education • Worship • Religious
Worldview • Professional Networks •
Experience • Art and Hobbies • Education •
Worship • Religious Worldview • Professional
Networks • Experience • Art and Hobbies •
Education • Worship • Religious Worldview •

SELFHOOD

Dealing with Criticism

What about that high-voltage condemnation with which
all leaders must deal? Isn't burnout often the result of too
much criticism? Perhaps, but dealing successfully with

Gatling gun criticism depends on how we perceive ourselves. Goliath's criticism was the verbal attack of a giant on a teenager. How could anyone stand up to the biting criticism of Goliath (see 1 Sam. 17:42–43)?

In a lifetime of pastoring, I found that nearly every new program I introduced came under attack. Innovation is nearly always met by challenge. The number one response to all change is resistance and not just passive resistance. Sometimes an active resistance hounds us, confronts us, and threatens us. To survive active and vicious criticism demands that we know who we are.

We must also know how we got into the business of leading Christ's church in the first place. The answer to the first issue is that we are the Christ-redeemed children of God. In this affirmation, we recall that we are loved. The love of God does not keep leaders from losing, but it does keep them from seeing themselves as losers.

Criticisms can break us or create us. One of the characters in *Steel Magnolias* properly offers, "That which doesn't break us makes us stronger." J. Willard Marriott said, "Good timber does not grow with ease; the stronger the wind, the stronger the trees."[13]

Our beliefs are what keep us stable during storms of criticism. They alone provide us with ballast in the gales. But what are beliefs? Beliefs are guiding principles, but they also serve as filters to our world view. Beliefs are directions. They are like theater ushers who help us make our way down dimly lit aisles and find our proper row in the dark. Beliefs hold martyrs upright on flaming stakes. They steady the soul-weary servant of God in times when he or she seems friendless.

Jesus, in the Sermon on the Mount, said: "Anyone who is angry with his brother will be subject to judgment. Again, anyone who says to his brother 'Raca' is answerable to the Sanhedrin. But anyone who says, 'you fool!' will be in danger of the fire of hell" (Matt. 5:22, NIV). Why is Christ so severe in teaching us to deal kindly with others? Because in severe criticism we devalue the worth of someone for whom He died. Our harshness destroys.

Those leaders the world considers worthy may not deserve coerced respect. Worthy leaders have worth because God appointed them to be leaders. They know that their only inherent worth comes from God. They know God loves them, and who are any of us to despise whom God loves even if it is ourselves?

These days of the "me-generation" give us a fearful day in which to try to be a pastor. The stress levels of contemporary pastors are soaring. Today's preachers rarely hear any good news about themselves. How can such dehumanizing stress ever be overcome?

Anthony Robbins says that stress can be overcome in a twofold formula: "First, don't sweat the small stuff, and, secondly, remember, it's all small stuff."[14] No terse formula can sum up our every need. But much of the pain of leadership comes from pretty small stuff. We allow these petty pressures to destroy our self-perception.

God's calling deserves dignity and honor, and self-respect should come directly from this calling. Have we not been called to lead? Doesn't this call deserve some honor? I am not one to blindly exalt despotic pastoral authority. But let every layperson remember that the pastor has been called by God.

There is much disagreement circulating about pastoral authority. To be sure, there is an authority that attends the pastor's calling. But this is an authority of conferral and not seizure. Hebrews 13:17 is a call to "obey your leaders" (NIV). This is not the *jure divino* of pastoral power. No pastor is to have carte blanche entitlement. Still, this verse does summon all laypersons to remember that pastors need support if they are going to lead effectively. The second part of Hebrews 13:17 says that the pastor is to have respect so that the work "will be a joy, not a burden." But woe to all who would become ruthless in their calling! Authority is not the real issue of Hebrews 13:17; responsibility is the issue. The verse reminds leaders that they "must give account" for how they manage the flock of God.

Robbin's Laws
for
Overcoming Stress

LAW I

DON'T SWEAT THE
SMALL STUFF

LAW II

ALL STUFF IS
SMALL STUFF

An old parable tells of a monastery sign in a mountainous section of Italy. The sign before the monastery bore these four admonitions:

First, if a stranger comes to this monastery, you will share with him what you have.

Second, if he criticizes, listen. He may be sent by the Lord.

Third, if he becomes obstreperous, he shall be cast out.

Fourth, if he refuses to go, four strong monks shall explain to him the will of God.

This seems to me to be a tidy and useful plan for good leaders with strong self-perception to deal with all criticism in the parish.

The Issue of Reputation

Loss of reputation is ever the risk of really creative leadership. Leaders cannot lead without reputation. On the other hand, when reputation becomes a more primary concern than the task of leadership, all forward motion can stop. The leader's dreams may dissolve. What others think of us determines how well or poorly we lead. But moving the church successfully from point A to point B requires a great deal of congregational change. The greater their reluctance to change, the more the leader's reputation can be damaged. Almost every person who marks history endures long seasons of ill will and poor reputation.

There is a formula by which we can compute the worth of risking our reputation:

Loss Conjectured + What Might Be Achieved = The Worthiness of Risk.

This formula asks that we compute as reasonably as we can all possible elements of loss. We must set them against the glorious possibility of winning. On the basis of these two integers, we can decide whether to abort our mission or risk the venture. To be sure, no leader can lead without some risk. Those who carefully calculate the cost of losing will usually not lose. Still, no risk is foolproof and no good dream is 100 percent sure. "Only those who dare to fail greatly can ever achieve greatly," said Robert Kennedy.

Jesus said it is to be expected that all venturesome leadership risks reputation. "Woe to you when all men speak well of you" (Luke 6:26, NIV). Or consider His grim prophecy about the committed, "You will be hated by all nations" (Matt. 24:9,

NIV). The cross of Christ is the focus for all who commit themselves to leadership. The cross proves that anytime we take ultimate steps to obey God, human opinion can move swiftly against us. But Jesus reminds us that all His followers from time to time must deal with wounded reputations. We best exonerate our leadership by reckoning ourselves dead to our ambition (Rom. 6:11). They who crucify themselves have nothing to lose (Luke 9:23; Gal. 2:20).

Once we have given up all rights to reputation, we may begin the walk of faith with nothing crucial to be lost! In commenting on Romans 6:11, Francis of Assisi asked: "Is Christ pleased?" If He is, and it can be determined that He is, there are no other consequential challenges to our leadership.

Conclusion

While we will talk later about the leader as a role model in the community he is leading, for now let us conclude this chapter by saying that the point of a leader's self-study is to celebrate his or her strong points sufficiently to lead strongly. Leading in strength always comes from a strong self-image. A strong self-image always is the basis of personal worth. Joe Batten counsels all of us when he counsels himself, "I will make the lives of others richer by the richness of my own."[15]

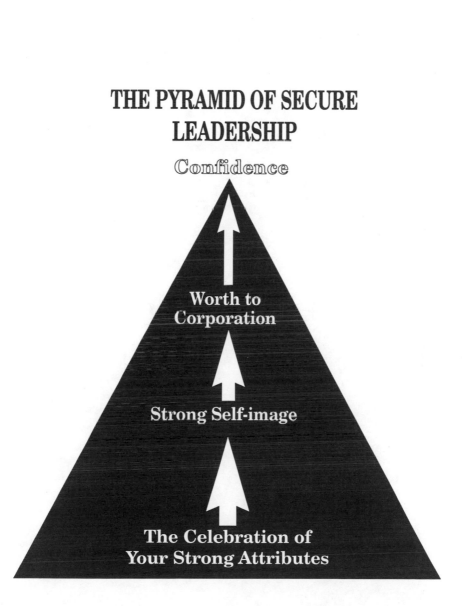

THE PYRAMID OF SECURE LEADERSHIP

Confidence

Worth to Corporation

Strong Self-image

The Celebration of Your Strong Attributes

KEY 3

Networking and the Special Friends of a Leader

Relations with peers
are enormously difficult
for the person aspiring
to supreme leadership.

James MacGregor Burns,
Leadership

I hope when I die
there will be at least five of my friends
who will be able to sit through my funeral
without looking at their watches.

The leader of a
large Christian organization
to R. C. Sproul

We sip the foam of many lives.

Ralph Waldo Emerson

Letter 3

Dear Leader:

I have always been fascinated by nets—at least, by two kinds of nets. I like the kind that catch fish and the kind that catch falling trapeze artists. The first net makes it possible for fishers to eat. The second makes it possible for aerialists to fall and stay alive. Great Christian leaders have always been interested in both kinds of nets. Jesus expected us to fish for men (Matt. 4:19), and the net is perhaps a dominant New Testament symbol of our calling. But while pastors serve they must also live on congregational pedestals of lofty visibility and danger.

Networking implies that leaders can join together to help each other with matters of productivity and career safety. By networking, pastors can share ideas on how to become more productive. But even more than this, they can help hold the nets that protect the lives and reputations of their friends. When the network works as it should, our peers will also be there holding the net for us in our time of need.

I know you're my leader and I'm your follower. But I am willing to be so much more. Would you consider being my friend? a real part of my network? If so, I am more than willing to be a part of yours. I don't know that I'd be much of a help to you. But I'd sure give it the old one-two. Before you join me, I need to tell you that I can be a real nuisance to my friends. I've got a real inferiority complex. Sometimes my nets come up empty for a long time, and I am plagued by worthless feelings of non-productivity. Not only that, but I often feel like I'm about to take the plunge from the pinnacle of my little successes. Frankly, I need a lot of propping up. I'm terribly insecure. Are you? If you want me, I'll be there holding the net for you. Will you be there for me?

—Your Follower

1 Samuel 18:1–4; 20:1–5, 8, 20–22

A great leader is never a Lone Ranger. Every leader knows that leadership is team stuff! All those who follow must also lead from time to time. This cooperative team playing comprises the network. Many current motivators use the word network to speak of that matrix of relationships that provide the people resources for individual success. Behind every dynamic man is the supporting confidence and help of his family. In a similar way, behind every great leader there is always a loyal network of a great many friends. Lee Buck, the one-time vice-president of New York Life, reminds us: "Making friends along the way is an action anyone pursuing success in his work should follow. This means being a friend to everyone, all fellow employees above and below you, even to those who you feel can do you absolutely no favors."[1]

A network allegiance to the leader is foundational to all he or she achieves. The leader who is a network leader is what Robert D. Dale calls a *catalyst leader*. Dale's four kinds of leaders are the catalyst, the commander, the hermit, and the encourager. Of these four kinds of leaders the catalyst leader is the most effective in building a team-driven church. The commander style of leader tends to be too autocratic. The hermit leader tends to be too withdrawn. The encourager leader is a counselor and friend but often not strong in management skills. Great leaders never forget the people who make their leadership possible. Thus the catalyst leader creates from these friends a strong command and a team agenda.[2]

In the passages listed above, David and Jonathan not only become friends, but their friendship pledged itself in marvelous allegiance. Without Jonathan, David might have been killed by the king's assassins. Had that happened, Israel's greatest light would have been extinguished.

Quality in leadership demands that you build a circle of loyal friends who will compose the network out of which

Bob Dale's
FOUR LEADERSHIP STYLES

STYLE	STRENGTH	WEAKNESS
Catalyst	Team Builder	Insignificant
Commander	Inspires Action	Autocratic
Hermit	Wise	Aloof
Encourager	Couselor	Poor Manager

(and upon which) your leadership can reach for excellence. To some, however, the word network implies that friends are only things to be used rather than persons to be served. No view of friendship could be more debilitating and unChristian. Remember, Jesus said to His disciples, "I no longer call you servants. . . . Instead, I have called you friends" (John 15:15, NIV). Did Jesus call us friends because He conceived us to be a part of some malleable network He could shape for His own selfish ends? Certainly not! Since Christ is our model, we should never view our network as something to be massaged for our self-interests.

Robert Dale's leadership styles are applicable to networking as a style of ministry, but consider the four leadership styles suggested by Ken Blanchard:[3]

Four Leadership Styles

Style 1: Directing

The leader provides specific instructions and closely supervises task accomplishment.

Style 2: Coaching

The leader continues to direct and closely supervise task accomplishment, but also explains decisions, solicits suggestions, and supports progress.

Style 3: Supporting

The leader facilitates and supports subordinates' efforts toward task accomplishment and shares responsibility for decision-making with them.

Style 4: Delegating

The leader turns over responsibility for decision-making and problem-solving to subordinates.

The most effective networking style is the coaching-supporting model. These styles will help you build an organization by trusting in your network of friends.

Judith Viorst suggests there are six categories of friends: convenience friends, special interest friends, historical friends, crossroads friends, cross-generational friends, and close friends.[4] These categories are rather self-explanatory, and David must have had friends in all six categories. Certainly all categories comprise the supportive circle we call our network.

What is more significant than David's friendship with Jonathan? David determined that his friendship with God would be the real priority in his life. We evangelicals often sing, "What a friend we have in Jesus." This hymn presumes we are considering our friendship with God a category six friendship—close. Emilie Griffin makes a dynamic statement about our friendship with God as a friendship of adoption, not a friendship of the flesh. She cites Shakespeare's words: "Those friends thou hast, and their adoption tried, Grapple them to thy soul with hoops of steel." Griffin then concludes that the grappling is done not by us, but by grace.[5]

The very word election implies that God first did the choosing to be friends with us. Our choosing God is important, but it comes later than His choosing us. As a potential leader, all of us must have important friends in category six. Such friends are indispensable to our success. It is touching that Lee Iacocca cited his barber as one of his close friends during a time of great stress. Every leader has friends who often do not measure up to the standards of social, political, or economic leadership but who serve behind the scenes in critical ways.

Our friendship with God is rooted in a paradox. We reach to God as we seek to maintain a critical balance—the balance between intimacy and awe. Sometimes, out of great respect, we sing, "Praise, my soul, the King of heaven." At other times, focused on our intimacy with Christ, we sing, "What a friend we have in Jesus." Which song expresses our friendship with God? Both, of course! In the balance between awe and intimacy, you celebrate a friend whose power to help you is as great as His personal interest in your life.

In this passage, David and Jonathan affirm their love for each other. In a sexually ambiguous world, some evangelicals have steered away from all talk of a love "surpassing the love of women" (2 Sam. 1:26). Still, here at the onset of David's reign, we need to see how much he owed Jonathan and his other friends. The others never reached David's pinnacle of historical importance, but without them David's place in history could never have come to be.

The Chemistry of Friendship

Knitting: Becoming One with Fellow Dreamers and Riskers

One characteristic of us who lead is our need for a matrix of support for all our dreams and visions. These dreams and support systems need the constant stimulation of our friends affirming us, hearing words like, "you're doing the right thing!" Those who comprise our network should be allowed to affirm us until our dreams seem reasonable to us. Without such affirmation, our dreams may remain unsure. In every situation where a CEO is making giant strides in his or her company, there is a surrounding battery of persons who give positive feedback about the quality and brilliance of his or her decisions.

Feedback is meant to offer correction for the steerage of leadership. Feedback is like the compass by which a ship on sunless days corrects the sail and rudder to be sure it is sailing in the right general direction. However, no ship ever sails in a straight line. It moves between corrected settings of port and starboard to zigzag its way along what appears to be a straight course. A thousand corrections of rudder and sail make the right course possible. All progression is determined by feedback and correction.

Leadership networks rarely exist in the church, and when they do, they often degenerate into directionless chumminess. Such networks are really leaderless. E. Stanley Jones comments about this: "We have classes for leadership in our churches—a mistake. This does not produce leaders—it only produces fussy managers and other people."[6]

Leadership rarely comes from community congeniality. On the contrary, a leader's genius lies in two directions: *the dreaming genius* and *the risking genius*. The dreaming genius requires support to maintain the dreams. But Philip Greenslade says that leadership is a collective noun.[7] Leadership never travels alone. The risking genius of a real leader requires daring followers who instill within him the courage to risk.

The late A. W. Tozer was fond of talking about two kinds of fellowship in the church. One kind of fellowship he called "front-line fellowship" and the other "rear-guard fellowship." At the back of a military advance, the generals sit having tea and discussing what might be the best strategies for the war at the front. But at the front there is no time for tea and speculation. There the bullets fly and the foxholes are never quite deep enough. There soldiers defend each other in a kind of camaraderie and fellowship impossible to those who, at the rear of the advance, munch cookies and sip tea. On the front line, criticism flies as thick as bullets. There the chemistry of friendship knits leaders and followers so closely that their dreams fall or stand together.

Clicking

But how are we to select a network of helpers? How are we to make these critical decisions that move us and our organization ahead? J. Paul Getty says there are five qualities we should seek to develop in ourselves, and these five qualities must always belong to those who comprise our network. "Alertness, imagination, enthusiasm, ambition, business acumen—these are among the characteristics that help make a beginner a desirable applicant."[8] Our supporting network should include these characteristics if they are going to contribute to the force of our leadership.

I have often asked those who lead companies what qualities they seek when hiring people. Philosophically they will often talk of how they hire to their "weaknesses" or how they hire people whose résumés are strong. But if you ask them candidly to tell you the final criteria they use in hiring, they will talk about chemistry. Basically, CEOs hire those with whom they "click." Clicking is a kind of romantic notion in hiring. It seems to stand opposite to the hard-course work of studying résumés. Yet basically, résumés only state qualifications. They say nothing about relationships. It's an unusual person who will hire someone with whom they feel no sense of relationship, no click. Most of us want to be involved with those whom we "like."

Avoiding the Yes-Man Syndrome

The yes-man may be nice in an organization, but he also never causes it to question itself, thus enabling it to grow. The network must be comprised of lovers, not gentlemen. Lovers want what's best for the organization. Gentlemen merely offer accord. Lovers confront in order to better their world. Gentlemen smile and abdicate.

There are many levels of chemistry in friendship. Chemistry is most valid when friendships can thrive without constant affirmation. It is always easy to see in a company how those who cluster around subordinate heads of power will appear to be in complete agreement with their superiors. Some see this as a form of job security, and some see this as currying favor with the powers that be. But the strongest people we really want to involve in our network are the people who can say "no" to us. The leader who has to surround himself with yes-people is not building a creative corporation. Neither can a leader who insists that the staff agree at every point contribute to overall growth of the organism. Speaking of the need for diversity of opinion in an organization, Max DePree says, "Diversity of opinion is as necessary as light and air, a diversity of opinion that is encouraged and exploited for the good of the group."[9]

Reading the Vibes

One of the things that the chemistry of friendship allows is the ability to listen not only to what people say but to "read the vibes and know what they mean." That leader is obtuse who has no awareness of body language. Staff people express their true struggle in a variety of non-verbal ways. The shifting of the feet, the nodding of the head, the deadness of the light in the eye—each of these movements are translatable to those who know how to read relationships.

Those who do not see anything more than superficial conversations will never build a suitable network. But when good friends work together over a long period of time, they develop an inner link to each other's moods, positions, viewpoints, and psychologies. To the sensitive, reading these vibes soon becomes unnecessary. All moods themselves are nearly telepathic. Networks feel a common status and viewpoint on widely diverse issues. This describes the glorious chemistry of friendship at its most basic and trusting level.

The Chemistry of Oneness

There are, it seems to me, three distinct levels of oneness that we achieve through the chemistry of friendship. There is, first of all, a oneness of leadership. This oneness vows, "I am with you and the corporation." Leadership oneness lays out before all those who are linked in network the strong feeling that the person who leads is to be respected and his or her directions followed. The second kind of oneness is a oneness of community. Community

The Three Varieties
of
CORPORATE ONENESS

Leadership Oneness — We Stand With the Leader

Community Oneness — We Stand With the Corporation

Spiritual Oneness — We don't stand with anyone. We belong to each other

oneness leads everyone in the corporate network to say, "This community is vital to my personal security and job satisfaction." Community oneness not only merely defends the leader but also the leader's ideals as they suffuse the entire community.

But the third and highest form of oneness is spiritual oneness. This oneness is not easily achievable. Spiritual oneness is one that seems to operate best between those who are Christian leaders. The core idea of this oneness is expressed succinctly in the Bible when Paul says it is by the Spirit that we know who our brothers are: "The Spirit himself testifies with our spirit that we are God's children" (Rom. 8:16, NIV). Spiritual oneness is indispensable to every network that dreams the noblest dreams of God.

The Shirt-off-My-Back Syndrome

In 1 Samuel 18:3–4, Jonathan literally gave David the shirt off his back. In truth, he gave David his tunic and cloak as a symbol. I suppose it is one thing to give someone the gift of a new garment. It is quite another thing to give them the very garment that we are wearing at the time. This gift expresses the high level of sacrifice that exists between good friends. The issue is one of high trust and confident delegation. This is especially true in that Jonathan also gave David his sword, his only means of self-defense. Jonathan's father had so long pursued David to put him to death, it was a generous act of trust for Jonathan to give David both his shirt and his sword.

In David and Jonathan, as pictured in 1 Samuel 18, we meet two people who are in some sense quite dissimilar. One of them is primarily a poet, the other strictly a warrior. Their relationship points out some very valid things that every leader wants to claim as a principle of networking. First of all, every leader wants to have some wonderful things in common with those who are part of the team. How much do most contemporary church leaders have in common with support staff? This question also presumes the question of how we hire when we want to fill staff vacancies in the organization. Again I emphasize first of all, we must always hire to our weaknesses. The friendship of David and Jonathan pointed out not only how they were different, but that differences can be exciting, even electric.

The depth of their friendship suggested that differences make an organization stronger, not weaker.

THREE PRINCIPLES
OF SOUND
NETWORKING

✓ **Having things in common with other team members**

✓ **Feeling comfort- able in either same or opposite gender relationships**

✓ **Allowing team members freedom to build other networks outside yours**

There's another kind of implication here. Most all of us need friends of the same sex. This truth is summed up in David's song after the battle of Mount Gilboa. He compliments Jonathan by saying, "Your love for me was wonderful, more wonderful than that of women" (2 Sam. 1:26,

NIV). To examine this verse is to understand that men need close male friends. Similarly, women need female friends. There is a level of trust in same-sex relationships that is both godly and important.

C. S. Lewis, in *The Four Loves,* talks about "need love" and "gift love." Need love is the love that we offer others to gain some reciprocity. Need love is also conditional. It is given only as long as there is some kind of response. Gift love is unconditional: it is the love that we give when there is virtually no response. Gift love is the kind of love a mother and father would give a retarded child. Such a love is often not returned in any tangible way throughout life. But most of us realize that in building networks, we tend to build networks out of those whose love is reciprocal.

Perhaps a word needs to be said in this section about how we must beware of bonding too tightly. It is perhaps not possible in the purest sense of the word to have too much bonding, but it is certainly possible to build relationships that become so demanding they hamper personal and corporate growth.

Such relationships can lead to jealousy. They foster suspicion and envy for all who enter into relationships outside the network. But gift love requires that we always set our friends free, giving them the right to lead within the organization.

Affirmation Within the Network

The One-Minute Manager is a book that makes it very clear that one of the strongest aspects of leadership is to find people doing something right and praise them for it. But there's more to affirmation than just praising someone who is doing a good job. The affirmation of great leaders also holds comrades responsible for their decisions. Basically, the affirmation of great leaders says, "I set you so free that you are free to make a mistake without that mistake costing you your job." I remember reading some years ago of an IBM executive who made such a mistake that it cost his company $3 million. He thought surely he would be fired. When the boss called him in to evaluate his costly debacle, he said to him, "I know you've been concerned about being fired but the truth is we have so much invested in you that we can't afford to let you go." It is that kind of attitude that builds health into a network.

Non-Possessive Leadership

We must never give others the impression that we are trying to build control by possessive leadership. I flinch every time I hear someone say, "*my* staff" or "*my* secretary." It is very important to grant people the dignity of their own individuality. We must allow team members to build their own social lives and have social freedom. It is a mark of insecurity and weakness when we build networks that we must control. When we structure our relationships so tightly that we don't allow those within our circle of friends to have friends other than ourselves, we sin against their freedom and dignity.

There is one other aspect of possessiveness even more difficult to honor. A great leader will allow team members to be friends with those who oppose him. As a pastor this was one of the hardest things for me to surrender. That some in my network of leadership might actually have one of my proven enemies as their close friend was at first unthinkable.

There's an insecurity among pastors as leaders that sometimes makes them want to over-control a congregation. The average pastor cannot allow people in his network to be friends with more staff than he can personally relate to or control. For this deplorable reason, we all have seen growth plateau in many churches. How sad! Pastors must select staff members and set them free to build their own networks within the church community.

Avoiding Oaths

Jesus said that we ought to let our "yea" be "yea" and our "nay" be "nay" (Matt. 5:37). Perhaps then, in directing a church we ought to be content to state our intentions and not our promises. We also ought to state only realistic goals. If we state our intentions rather than making promises, we'll never be guilty of disappointing our constituency. As we state realistic goals, we're making it possible for people to feel an important sense of group vision. However, the leader who never sets goals and agendas that the company can match is building a system of discord. No network, however loyal, will serve with vibrancy unless they feel the pride of achievement.

Conclusion

Lee Buck sums up the whole issue of networking in these words: "How one treats others in his or her climb up the ladder is vital. For each friend made along the way is a building block in your foundation of success."[10]

Vision:
Gathering It Up
and
Giving It Out

If your eye be single,
your whole body
will be full of light.

Jesus of Nazareth,
"The Sermon on the Mount"

Did you know
that studies have shown
it is almost impossible to give a dog an ulcer?
Do you know why?
Because dogs hardly every try
to be anything but a dog.

Steve Brown,
No More Mr. Nice Guy

For the man who cannot wonder,
is but a pair of spectacles behind which there is no eye.

Thomas Carlyle

Letter 4

Dear Leader:

Have you ever been in Carlsbad when they turned the lights out? Well, I was once. I wouldn't want to do it again, but I'm glad I did it once. I learned a great lesson there: the only place you can be when the lights go out is in the dark. I sure was glad the tour guide stayed by the light switch.

I've belonged to churches where I felt like I was in the dark, and nobody knew where the switch was. We didn't dare try to move ahead because we didn't know which way was ahead.

I think I'm pretty much like everybody else. I want to see where I am going. To be a leader you really need two things: a flashlight and an index finger. The light keeps it from being dark, and the finger points the way.

There is one other thing that helps—a picture. Keep the lights on, and point with the index finger at the picture of what I am supposed to be looking for. That way I will have a clear idea of where I am going. To be honest I really want to go. I'm tired of where I am and I want to keep moving. So show me the picture and give me the light and point the way. No need to look around. I'll be right behind you.

—Your Follower

2 Samuel 5:1–10

Decision making authenticates leadership. But making decisions that are realistic empowers leadership. Max DePree said in a Peter Drucker interview that a leader must have vision, for leaders are often future-oriented. DePree distinguished between vision and future-orientedness: "Those are not exactly the same things. To talk more specifically about the duties of a leader, I happen to believe that the first duty of a leader is to define reality. Every organization, in order to be healthy, to have renewal processes, to survive, has to be in touch with reality."[1] The church today hungers for visionary leaders whose dreams are tempered with a genuine understanding of the way things really are.

The entire industrialized complex huddles around the word *vision*. Walter Heller, interviewed by *Nation's Business*, was asked, "What do you think makes good leaders?" He replied that the two things leaders had to own were courage and vision. "These are sheer essentials," he said.[2]

Vision is the word to drop if you want immediate attention from either managers or planners. Literally thousands of visioning conferences are sponsored by the CEOs of America's important, thriving corporations. But what does the word *vision* literally mean? Vision is the photographic image that guides a pilgrimage to the goal it depicts. Proverbs 29:18 reads, "Where there is no vision the people perish" (KJV). John Haggai contributes to our understanding of this verse when he reminds us that the "true meaning of these words is, that without a vision, the people cast off restraint. When a group is under the direction of a person who has no vision, the result is confusion, disorder, rebellion, uncontrolled license, and—at worst—anarchy."[3] Most contemporary CEOs would agree with Proverbs 29:18. Dynamic leadership is always fueled by vision as the word is defined in Scripture.

Gunnar Myrdal once said that Americans worship success.[4] This is probably true. While it is hard not to admire it, wherever success exists it is vision that creates it. So let us begin by trying to understand the nature of vision in general. Does vision seem too grand a word to apply to your own life or career? How do you get vision? Where does it come from? Karl Jaspers was an existential philosopher who taught that all living, to be meaningful, had to touch some "axial point." This axial point may come as a crisis of personal pain. But even periods of pain may bring us a new vision that redefines our lives.

But *pain* may be too mild a word. Often vision comes as the result of some tearing circumstance by which we come to an end of our own ability to make life work. But we are never to deplore such times! In the darkness of such times, we may achieve a breakthrough. This breakthrough may come as an exhilarating insight. Such illuminating insights are symbolized by the Ford Motor Company with its "better-idea" light bulb. It may be a laser of hope that slices through your gray existence and illuminates some new direction—a clear glory you had not been able to see before the pain came. That illumination may become the conveyance to Jaspers' axial point.

I believe we can exercise what I like to call four axioms of judgment to turn our reversals into opportunities.

1. Nothing happens to us by accident; all reversals are God-given challenges sent to transfer our complacency to passion.

2. Never sidestep challenges. Grab every charging bull by the horns and slap him twice across the face. Remind him that God is in charge of you, and you're in charge of him.

3. Love people, use things. Never, ever reverse this order or you will become inhuman and unworthy of the high character of God's servants.

4. Don't celebrate leisure and condemn hard work. Put leisure and labor side by side, and esteem them both. Leisure will give your life pacing. Labor will make you productive.

If you can remember these four beliefs you will find your vision survives all challenges. Then even reversals can sharpen your vision.

One thing is sure: without some painful axial point and its subsequent new vision, life for most of us is mundane. Visionless living provides no real *raison d'être* (reason to be). Vision may be the only valid escape from aimlessness. "After his conversion to Marxism in 1963, [playwright Peter] Weiss stated that the effect of aimlessness in the West was to destroy at the root, all cultural and creative activity."[5] Vision is as important to nations as it is to individuals.

It is important to understand three things about the nature of vision: first, its inherent power; second, where it comes from; and finally, how you hold on to it.

First, consider the inherent power of vision. Its dynamic is the enthusiasm it infuses. The enthusiasm inspired by vision results in some kind of life product. Feelings of productivity increase your feelings of self-esteem, causing a healthy celebration of your usefulness to God and your world. A former NCR employee described vision this way: "Genius is intensity. The salesman who surges with enthusiasm, though it is excessive, is superior to the one who has no passion. I would prefer to calm down a geyser than start with a mudhole."[6] The power of enthusiasm is the energy that drives every successful idea. And enthusiasm has its taproot in the fertile soil of vision. We will see shortly how all of this operated in the life of David of Israel.

But where does vision come from? Ralph Neighbour Jr. says that the seven first words of the church are, "I can do all things through Christ."[7] Surely Christ is the fount of our best imagination and vision. The finest visions that can possess us come directly from God through Christ. But I must sound this word of warning. God does not shout His best vision through hassled Christian living. It is in the quiet that He gives the most delivering visions of life. John Haggai's own creed of real success:

> You can't see a vision when the artificial lights of the Broadways, the Rialtos, and the commercial offices of the world blind your eyes, any more than you can see the stars at night when you are standing in New York's Times Square, Tokyo's Ginza, or London's Picadilly Circus.
>
> You are more likely to discern a vision in the cloistered halls of solitude than in the screaming jostle of the metropolitan concrete jungle. Perhaps in the cathedral of the trees, under the silence of the stars, or by the moaning sea, you'll be most likely to see the true light and hear "the still, small voice."[8]

In a similar way, psychologist Nathaniel Branden wrote: "Innovators and creators are persons who can, to a higher degree than average, accept the condition of aloneness. They are more willing to follow their own vision even when it takes them far from the mainland of the human community."[9] Alan Loy McGinnis reminds us that Jesus' life was checkered with solitude.[10]

The third thing we must discover is how to keep vision alive. Holding on to a redeeming vision through all kinds of trials can be hard. New visions burn brighter than old ones. In the press of your days and years, old dreams first lose their fire, then the enthusiasm they once supplied. A wealthy American immigrant sadly testified, "I heard that in America there was a pot of gold at the end of the rainbow. I found the gold but I lost the rainbow." Clinging to rainbows can be an arduous task.

What is the leader's rainbow? It is the finalized picture of where the leader wants to be when he or she has arrived at the pinnacle of meaning. *Self-meaning* is a better term to describe the goals of visionaries than success. But Anthony Robbins says there are seven basic mechanisms that can ensure success. They are passion, belief, strategy, clarity of values, energy, network rivalry, and mastery of communication.[11]

I have read very few books on leadership that do not see communication as a key part of visionary leadership. John Kenneth Galbraith went so far as to say, "Money is what fueled the industrial society. But in the informational society, the fuel, the power, is knowledge. One has now come to see a new class structure. . . . This new class has its power not from money, not from land, but from knowledge."[12] Knowledge is the stuff of communication, and Robbins agrees that communication is power. "Those who have mastered its effective use can change their own experience of the world and the world's experience of them. . . . Think of the people who have changed our world—John F. Kennedy, Thomas Jefferson, Martin Luther King Jr., Franklin Delano Roosevelt, Winston Churchill, Mahatma Gandhi. . . . What these men all had in common was that they were master communicators."[13] Vision plus communication is the winning profile of leadership. Those who can articulate their vision become for God a fulcrum with which He moves the world.

Perhaps it needs to be said that your visions will serve you best, not when you keep them, but when they keep *you*. I want to suggest two ingredients for the recipe of vision keeping. Number one is an adequate quiet time. When you are quiet before the altar of your own trust in God, vision will hold a strong place in your life. Visions grow in quietness, never in the hurry and noise of life. A second ingredient of vision keeping is rehearsal. You must constantly rehearse your dreams. It is never enough to claim that you rehearsed them in the past and that you have memorized their form. Visions require a central altar in our continuing lives. They must be a part of each new day, or soon they will not keep faith with *any* day. A couplet of my own reads: "Old promises must pledge themselves each day or, unrenewed, pass quietly away."[14]

Now let us examine the life of David of Israel and see what we can learn from his vision tending that may supply vitality to your own. George Barna describes David this way: "David became the second King of Israel, described as a man after God's own heart. Or, put another way, David was a man who had grasped God's vision for his life, a man whose service and worship exemplified the spirit and commitment of a person in relationship with God. . . . David was human and, as such, made mistakes. But one of his redeeming qualities was his burning desire to remain true to the vision or the future that God had placed in his heart, which God allowed him to work toward despite the frailties of his human nature."[15]

Vision is a dream inebriated by imagination, and "a dynamic imagination has the power to change what is found, to shift the information and bring the best results."[16]

David was a man of vision. In 2 Samuel 5:1–10 he took a giant step in favor of a powerful symbol, Zion, Jerusalem. David's city—the citadel—came to be idealized as Zion, the utopian city of God. Martin Luther King once cried before a massive audience in Washington, D.C., "I have a dream!" Dreams are characteristic of all world-changers. David, too, had a dream. He envisioned a city that would be the center of God's presence in the world. Jerusalem would never have existed apart from the power of his vision. Great vision serves leadership in four ways.

Vision Unites

In 2 Samuel 5:3 the statement is made that "all the elders of Israel . . . anointed David king over Israel" (NIV). This is probably an overstatement. There's rarely ever been a time in the history of any nation, corporation, or church when the entire organization came together. Still, for all practical purposes, it was so. A large crowd, certainly the majority of the nation, seems to have come together to crown David king.

I used to hear evangelists say that if all the people of the church would trust God, He would send a great revival. The statement is not blatantly false, but it waits on the best truth. Not everybody in the church has to agree on the dream to have progress. In fact, sometimes if only a few people intensely want a revival, the visitation of God will surely come. While vision pulls people together, there's rarely ever been a vision so all-encompassing it united everyone.

Every vision by definition is new. Any raging vision seems new, and its very newness claims the attention of the group. In fact, vision is destroyed by a sense of aging. As visions grow older they tend to become wearisome clichés. Not only do the visions themselves get old but the promotion around them begins to yellow with age. But there's no such thing as an old vision. If the vision is motivating, however old it is, it will appear to be new. Thus it will enthuse and draw together a people as though indeed it had just come into existence.

In many cases, a founding vision for a church may remain the same over twenty or thirty years. Perhaps that vision is to reach a particular community and the church will begin to grow. Many churches have grown over the years spurred on by their initial visions. The First Baptist Church of Dallas, in a period of eighty years, only had two pastors and still it continued to grow.

As aging kills vision, enthusiasm connotes newness. But beware of adding amendments to any dream. Such restrictions usually slow and sometimes kill a vision. The most powerful visions remain simple at heart. The more we try to amend simple visions, the less visionary they become. Amendments assassinate vision. George Barna is concise in this proverb: "For the vision to be effective . . . it must be simple enough to be remembered and specific enough to give direction."[17]

Visions find such frequent amendment in institutions. Their unique power is clotted and mired down by those good ideas that are married to the simple vision to be sure that everybody gets in on the action. Beware those who seek to amend a simple dream. Warren Bennis calls us to heed his two laws of *Pseudodynamics*. Law one states, "Routine work drives out nonroutine work and smothers to death all creative planning." Law two continues, "The trivial always displaces the grand."[18]

Old line denominations characterized American religion until the middle sixties when they began to fail. The rapid growth of the independent, evangelical churches of America came in and usurped the former glory of the older denominations. Why? Because the independent evangelicals were composed of single dreamers who didn't have to please heavily structured, bureaucratic denominations. Dreaming cannot easily slog through the mire of denominational officiendo. Red tape wraps dreams in small packages.

Third, it must be said that while vision does unite, it may also divide. Every founding vision has people who champion it, but every founding vision also is a cry for change. Change inevitably brings some resentment and division. Vision often divides because it calls for changes that eliminate petty self-interests. Still, a strong vision fuels healthy organization with community spirit. It keeps the church rehearsing its reason for existence.

Vision Always Provides a Call for Focus

In 2 Samuel 5:5 David began his reign in the south. David never considered his rule over southern Israel to be permanent. He had a dream of moving the capital of Israel into the fortress of Jebus, which he would later name Jerusalem, the city of God. Vision funnels wide interests into narrow channels. It is much like the Colorado River moving swiftly through the tall gorges of the Grand Canyon. When a river is wide it dawdles lazily across a plain. But where the river narrows into white water channels, its force becomes capable of moving a great deal of water very rapidly through a very narrow canyon.

Vision gathers multiple, complex organizations into single goal relationships. A vision's power derives directly from the simplicity of its definition. When the focus of vision narrows, like a canyon cutting river, the dynamics of the dream rush forward. On the other hand, the longer it takes a leader to state his or her vision for an organization, the more the complex dream slows to a meandering focus.

Peter Drucker said we are witnessing the death of the large corporation. Those corporate giants, like large denominations, tend to trade the compelling simplicity of their vision for a killing complexity. "The flagships of the last 40 years, institutions like General Motors, ITT and Du Pont, have basically outlived their usefulness. . . . They're past their peaks. There's very little flexibility there, very little creativity. . . . You know, elephants don't do well in confined spaces. Their ability to wriggle through a hole in the wall is very small. You'd be better to be a rat."[19]

The word *vision* and the word *see* are related. If people cannot see, there is no vision. One of the best things any leader can do is to create simple pictures of organizational dreams and goals. But the leader cannot create these dreams and goals if they are not first pictorial in the leader's mind. Without clearly drawn maps to the future, the organization remains hamstrung by the past.

Through four different church building programs, I realized how very important it was for the people of the church to see pictures—proposed drawings or artists' models—of the new buildings as they would look when finished. One picture may not be worth a thousand words, but one picture will furnish a whole congregation a seeable, attainable dream.

Vision Dominates All Inner Conversation

In 2 Samuel 5:6 one can imagine the citizens of Jebus, called Jebusites, taunted David that he could never take their city. The walls were too high, the gates were too formidable, the topography too forbidding. But the more the Jebusites said to David, "You will not get in here; even the blind and the lame can ward you off " (2 Sam. 5:6, NIV), the more David drove himself to do what they said couldn't be done. But the taunts of the Jebusites only armored this king's intentions. The path of David's siege was paved with the jeers of Jebusites. The Jebusites awakened the king's intentions and set his dreams to hurry his resolve. Great visions always dominate a leader's inner conversation. "The leader cherishes his vision. He thinks on it day by day and dreams of it at night."[20]

Though many feel Psalm 24 is quite late in biblical history, I would rather believe that it truly is a Psalm of David. I like believing David wrote it before entering Jebus. Therefore, I am warmed by the thought that Psalm 24 does not celebrate that time when he brought the ark of the covenant into the city. It is a psalm of glorious prophecy. This psalm is not the report of the siege, it rather rehearses a life dream. David, in this Psalm, sees past the Jebusites threat. His is the dream that the ark would one day enter Jerusalem. On that day God would open the great gates of Jebus with the cry: "Lift up your heads, O ye gates . . . and the King of glory shall come in" (Ps. 24:7, KJV). David's vision of this event made it possible for him to paint that vision for others.

Every worthy vision dominates some leader's inner conversation. It is best never to place great dreams in the hands of fanatics. Radicals distort the power of simple images. They over-emotionalize them and mar their shapes. Further, radicalism attracts extremists. Extremists are hard to handle. Ultimately extremists replace simple visions with modified agendas.

Still the glory of leadership demands that they make their visions pictorial. When their vision becomes too hot to keep, it breaks upon the group. Then they dominate the inner conversation. Dreaming a single dream is motivational single-mindedness. It releases the force of leadership wherein enthusiasm sets the organization free.

Visions Inspire Greatness

In 2 Samuel 5:7 there's a clear indication that David's vision inspired images of greatness. Some years ago Ernest Becker won the Pulitzer prize for his book *The Denial of Death*. It was the contention of Becker's book that people in our society deny their own death by taking one of two courses. They either decide to become a hero and thus live on after they are dead. Or, they may, by contrast, attach themselves to very strong heroes and thus transcend their littleness. As a hero lives forever, so hero worshippers also transcend death.

Conclusion

The greatness of personal vision is important to any group. The more electric and driving a vision is, the more it will inspire greatness in all those who hold it. Visions, by giving a picture of our place in the future, confer upon us a sense of dignity. This dignity demands that there be a place in our organization for our dreams. When our dreams match those of the organization, an important loyalty is born. This group faith allows the organization to move forward with zeal and meaning, both for the leader and those he or she has rallied to the dream.

Decision:
The Key to Leadership

It ain't nothin' 'til I call it.

An American umpire

Two roads diverged in a wood, and I—
I took the one less traveled by,
And that has made all the difference.

Robert Frost,
"The Road Not Taken"

Leaders,
whatever their professions of harmony,
do not shun conflict;
they confront it,
exploit it,
ultimately embody it.

James MacGregor Burns,
Leadership

Letter 5

Dear Leader:

It was Miss Smith, my third grade teacher that first taught me about mug-wumps. They're real hard to describe, so I won't try. It's just enough that you know that they spend all of their lives straddling fences. I can't imagine a more neurotic way to live, can you? There they sit, year after wishy-washy year with their mugs sticking out on one side of the fence and their . . . well, never mind.

I know why mug-wumps avoid decision-making. Deciding is risky. Every single time you do it, you run the risk of being wrong. Of course, you also have a wonderful opportunity of being right. Either way, however, deciding seems to me less frustrating than having to live in that self-imposed state of paralysis known as decidophobia.

Miss Smith also taught me two nursery rhymes. One was about a lightning bug and one, a centipede. I still remember both of them.

> *A lightning bug lives most confused.*
> *He hasn't any mind.*
> *He wanders through existence*
> *With his headlight on behind.*

But I really like the one about the centipede best.

> *The centipede was happy quite*
> *Until the toad in fun said,*
> *"Pray, which leg comes after which?"*
> *Which worked her mind to such a pitch*
> *She fell distracted in the ditch*
> *Considering how to run.*

There's no question about it, the safest of all courses is to doubt. But, while it's the riskiest, the most exciting of all courses is decision. Doubters often live bored; deciders never.

Anyway, Pastor, make a decision and take off. I'll follow you even if your decision is wrong. I'd just as soon go the wrong direction now and then, as never go anywhere.

—Your Follower

2 Samuel 6:1–15; 7:1–13

Leaders are decision makers. Most of us quail before the lonely work of decision making. We take the struggle out of our work by making clear-cut decisions. Leaders are deciders. They create piers in oceans of alternatives by saying yes or no.

Throughout Israel's wilderness sojourn, the ark of the covenant was located in the Tabernacle. It was the central altarpiece of the Exodus experience. The tents, shanties, and portable lean-tos of Israel were gathered around the ark. Thus the ark, and the God who hovered above its mercy seat, became a certain center in Israel's uncertain forty years of sojourn.

In this passage we see that Israel has a proud new capital, Jerusalem, the "city of peace." But David realized it would become a city of turmoil without God's direction. The ark of the covenant symbolized God's presence on earth. As it presided in the wilderness tabernacle, it must have been housed within Jerusalem. Only as the ark remained central in the nation could every decision be made in the secure knowledge that God was not peripheral to what was occurring.

Like all great leaders, David was decisive. For him, all decision making began and ended with God. His need to move the ark into Jerusalem was based on his conviction that godly leaders make sound decisions only after they have consulted with God. David's great decision was to move the ark to the urban center of the nation. This pier decision formed a decisive bulwark on which he could build the smaller decisions of his monarchy. Making great decisions well makes easy the making of small decisions. Every leader must know how to recognize and make these pier decisions.

Pier decisions are those decisions that place God at the center of things. For the Christian, the first pier decision is to admit Christ into one's life and allow Him to take His rightful place of lordship. Evangelicals generally refer to this pier decision as "making a decision for Christ." You very likely have already made such a decision. To admit Christ to His rightful place of lordship is to prepare yourself to make other, sound pier decisions. Figuratively, it is deciding to make the ark—the consultation of God—the chief counselor in your decision-making process.

For the real leader, pier decisions serve in four ways: (1) they divide life into manageable segments, (2) they create new beginnings, (3) they authenticate a strong sense of self, and (4) they weld us into a lifelong participation with God that leads to meaningful living.

Let us first consider how decisions divide life into manageable segments. David never forgot the day he brought the ark of the covenant into the holy city. It became for him a milestone in his long and productive reign. In a similar way, coming to Christ for the first time marks such a dividing of our lives. All that came before the decision is of ourselves. All that comes after it is of God. All that comes after it is profit. Marriage proposals and military enlistments are other decisions that mark the great divisions of our lives. By merely saying, "I do," we divide twenty years of singleness from fifty years of marriage. In a similar way, by saying, "Lord, I believe," we surrender the aimless years of our lostness to the meaningful years of Christ-directed living.

A second way pier decisions serve is by creating new beginnings. Your decisions, right or wrong, create places for you to start again. Certainly you have sometimes found life to be mundane or boring. In such drudging circumstances, a fresh start is always welcome. A good, firm decision can provide a starting place from which to choose a new direction.

One of the best ways decisions serve is to provide a strong sense of self. They do this by summoning, from your innermost being, the ego force necessary to make these awesome decisions. Certainly David must have received some criticism of his administrative decision to bring the ark into the holy city. But he acted in the face of criticism

THE FOUR FUNCTIONS
OF
PIER DECISIONS

 They divide life
into manageable
segments.

 They create new
beginnings.

They authenticate
selfhood.

 They weld us into a
strong relationship
with God.

and became a stronger person for having decided. To exercise personal courage is to become stronger.

Decisions also serve your sense of self by reminding you that you are responsible for your own life and fortune. Decisive lifestyles teach that to a large degree you create yourself. Brick by brick, as a mason builds a tower, you do indeed create who you are. The bricks that compose the tower of your life are the single decisions you have made. Together they comprise your collective destiny.

Finally, decisions create a sense of self by forcing you into the cauldrons of refining loneliness. Others may help you clarify decisions, but you must do your deciding alone. Obadiah Milton Conover wrote, "Alone I walk the peopled city where each seems happy with his own; O friends, I ask not for your pity—I walk alone."[1]

Yet the loneliness of decision making is not a desolate aloneness, but a reaching aloneness. Decisions make you a partner with God. The insecurity we feel in making decisions clearly shows us how much we long to be right, to be on God's side.

Somewhere around fifty percent of all decisions you make will be wrong. An intimate walk with God can help you lower this dreadful percentage. John Maxwell wrote that great decisions are often as much a matter of timing as event.[2]

As you examine the life of David, you will unearth the principles of decision making. Learn from them. Seek your own maturity in leadership by becoming responsibly decisive.

When we dredge up early decisions and "redecide" them, we serve only our doubts, not our certainty. Peter Drucker offers us wise counsel on this issue of "redeciding": "If at first you don't succeed, try once more, then do something else!"[3]

Keeping God close at hand will avoid a circuitous, indecisive life. Really, redeciding is an oxymoron. It is like speaking of a decisive drifter. Anytime we find ourselves passing the same scenery because we are "redeciding," our lives are uncertain. We have lost the map to destiny. God is absent from our counsel.

THE FOUR POSTULATES OF DECISION AND CONSEQUENCE

THE WRONG DECISION
AT THE WRONG TIME =

✓ **DISASTER**

THE WRONG DECISION
AT THE RIGHT TIME =

✓ **MISTAKE**

THE RIGHT DECISION
AT THE WRONG TIME =

✓ **REJECTION**

THE RIGHT DECISION
AT THE RIGHT TIME =

✓ **SUCCESS**

Good Decision Making Wants God Close at Hand

Great leadership always gets God involved in the process. Moses was met by his father-in-law during a time of great executive stress and given three pieces of advice.

1. *Talk more to God about the people than to the people about their problems.* Your wisdom would be worth more if you did, and some problems would disappear immediately (Exod. 18:20).

2. *Teach the people more clearly to walk in God's ways.* Many of them will stop being parasitic on your wisdom and good nature and will begin to stand on their own two feet, mature enough to discern for themselves between good and evil (Exod. 18:20).

3. *Delegate responsibility to others and share the burden of leadership with them* (Exod. 18:21).[4]

The essence of Jethro's trust-God-and-delegate advice is, "Don't be a Lone Ranger." Be sure that in your network of leadership, you include God and the most trustworthy of team players who can help you discern His will.

Servant leadership wants God close at hand. The ark of the covenant represented God's presence among His people. The ark was a portable altar. As such, it was an adjunct to that portable cathedral called the tabernacle. This portable altar was carried throughout the trials of Israel's sojourn in Sinai. God's own presence was believed to ride atop the ark. After David came to occupy Jerusalem (see 2 Sam. 6:2), so did the ark. In David's life, as in the life of Israel, God neither lingered behind them nor moved ahead of them. He was present.

I have a friend who became my friend only after I had led him to faith in Christ. He was the leader of a rather large company. Shortly after the night he received Christ, I visited the company he directed. When I walked into his office, I saw, laying conspicuously in the center of his desk, a very large Bible. I asked him, "Why such a large Bible?" He replied, "I've tried to run my life and my company too long without God. I want to try it His way from now on." I believe that he was deciding to move the ark of God into his corporate leadership. And he was saying loud and clear, "I want to lead with God very near at hand."

JETHRO'S AXIOMS

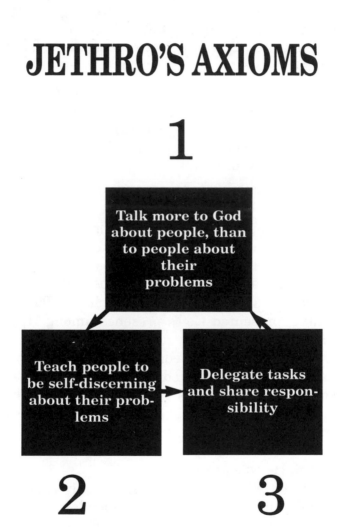

1

Talk more to God about people, than to people about their problems

Teach people to be self-discerning about their problems

Delegate tasks and share responsibility

2   **3**

Good Decisions Respect the Power of God

Our decisions gain ethical correctness when we respect the great power of God. The burden of having God close at hand is having to lead under the immense scrutiny of His holiness. Ecclesiastes 12:13 says that it is our duty to fear God. As we walk under the awe of His majesty, we experience the terror of acting in His behalf. Hebrews 12:29 reminds us that our God is a "consuming fire." This does not mean that we are ever to be immobilized by the fear of disappointing God with wrong decisions. Still, our respect for His majesty is ever to remind us of our inherent weaknesses. The only way that we can ever make strong decisions is to depend on Him.

Finding His will is always more difficult than acting on His behalf. But when we have prayed and hungered for insight, we must sometimes decide His decisions intuitively. The key to being sure that we are deciding as He directs lies sometimes in our desire to please Him. For when He seems to give us no clear answers, we must act out of our desire to please Him with our decisions. Our desire for His pleasure will sanctify our decisions. There are no mistakes possible to those who act beyond all self-interest. Still, it is tricky business. But how can we decide in strength while feeling so unsure of ourselves? And how, while we are in the midst of decision making, shall we ever be confident that we are making good decisions? I would like to look at those indicators that enable us to rate the quality of our decisions even as we are making them.

Three Indicators of Good Decision Making

In 2 Samuel 6:6–7, Uzzah is destroyed for touching the ark of the covenant. However you view this strange event, mark this: God is all-powerful, and His might is never to be taken for granted. Considering Uzzah's misfortune in touching the ark, we ourselves ought always to approach God with reverence and fear. Uzzah's fate should keep us from considering too flippantly that we have made good decisions that God will always honor. But what steps can we take to be sure that we have made good decisions that God will honor? I believe that there are three indicators that tell us we are making decisions that God can honor.

Good Decisions Are Made in an Atmosphere of Joy

The first indicator of good decision making is that we have made our decision, not in moments of self doubt, but in moments of worshiping the living God.

Second Samuel 6:14–15 tells the story of David's bringing the ark into the city. It was done in an atmosphere of great joy. David was so carried away he began dancing in excitement. Admittedly this kind of behavior is irregular for a CEO's management style. Further, David was immodestly attired in a too-short tunic. Some upper-class folk who were there doubtless criticized his immodest dancing. But there is a level of joy in decision making that creates fantastic enthusiasm. This ecstasy welds our followers together.

Every time I read this portion of the Bible, I feel drawn to David's enthusiasm. There is a wonderful kind of transport in "dancing decisions." David illustrates that the effervescence of dancing decisions is contagious. By contrast, poker-faced decisions, even if they are great decisions, gather support more slowly.

In four successive building programs of a church I pastored, I discovered that it was always good to subject my decisions to doubt. The negative scrutiny yielded great results and purified the deciding process. But when it came to getting the church on board to follow my vision, I knew my best decisions needed to be contagious. They needed to be "dancing decisions."

I also found there is only one good way to put the dance in dancing decisions: personal worship. I felt that to be sure I was leading the church into honest joy, I needed to spend private time in praising God. Following this "closet" praise, I needed to quit praising Him and spend some quiet time listening to God. Only after I had praised and He had spoken could I be sure that my joy was authentic.

Is it possible to make dancing decisions and lead the church soundly in such joy and hilarity? It is indeed. It is important for the good leader to be sure, as he or she can be, that they have the last word from God on the matter. But can we not at times make terrible mistakes, while joyously believing we are doing things right? Can those times not embarrass the whole community that we lead? Perhaps. Nonetheless, it is better to lead in joy, making occasional mistakes, than to try to lead with sterile data and cold logic. We must combine sound business acumen with spiritual insight.

But what of those times when we make big mistakes? Our reply to those times is to try to involve ourselves in the oft-futile activity of decision repair. We convince ourselves that if we bandage a poor decision we will heal. Then we can remake it into a good decision. Usually such is not the case. Peter Drucker wisely advises us: "This is how we've always done it. Let's improve it a little bit. This is one of the critical decisions. It is one of the crucial tasks of the executive to know when to say, 'Enough is enough. Let's stop improving. There are too many patches on those pants.'"[5] Deciding once and deciding well avoids such patchwork. Decision repair usually serves to keep us so busy with yesterday's decisions we avoid the dangerous work of making new ones.

Good Leadership Decides in Favor of God Before Self

In 2 Samuel 7:2 David felt bad that he had his own house, a permanent palace, before God had a house of His own. This kind of spiritual altruism inhabits the spiritual disciplines of prayer and Bible study. But where do prayer and Bible study themselves come from? I think these disciplines arise from our own spiritual neediness. Please remember that great leaders are not those who have worked their way up to personal confidence. Nor do they see themselves as God's ready achievers in this world. Spiritual leaders only appear to be giants to others. To themselves they are in desperate need of God.

amen

Abraham Lincoln, whom we now revere as the greatest of American leaders, confessed his neediness when he admitted, "I have been driven to my knees many times on the overwhelming conviction that I had nowhere else to go!" Paul the apostle readily lamented in 2 Corinthians 12:9–10, "Most gladly therefore will I rather glory in my infirmities, that the power of Christ may rest upon me. Therefore I take pleasure in infirmities, in reproaches, in necessities, in persecutions, in distresses for Christ's sake: for when I am weak, then am I strong" (KJV). There is no leader quite so powerful as a spiritually needy leader. There are no decision makers who make better decisions than those unsure leaders who must have God's help with deciding. But there is a third evidence that we are making good decisions.

Good Leadership Sometimes Makes Decisions to Postpone Deciding

Is this a real evidence for strong leadership? Wouldn't most people see this as a sign of weakness? Quite to the contrary, sometimes a very strong decider can strongly decide to postpone decisions. Such decisions may, in fact, be decisive. Lee Iacocca, in assuming control of Chrysler, decided not to decide on his salary for a whole year after taking control of a dying automobile corporation. He took only a dollar for his first year's salary and then proceeded to dismiss many top-level executives whose salaries were eating the heart out of Chrysler's profits. Was such a decision a real decision? Was it seen to be decisive? Yes is the obvious answer to both questions.

In 2 Samuel 6:10–12, following the accidental death of Uzzah, David decided to do nothing. This decision must have been approved of God. The house of Obed-Edom where the ark came to rest was blessed in that interim of David's indecision. Then when David had a clearer word from the Lord, he clearly decided to bring the ark into Jerusalem. His joyous dancing grew out of his postponed decision. He was just as decisive in postponing a decision as he was in dancing the ark into Jerusalem.

Decisions have a life of their own. They are like persons who change the face of history. Consider the great men and women who have lived decisive and courageous lives. If they had come a generation earlier or later, would they have meant as much to the world? Decisions gain nobility from their context in time. There are two all important rules for deciding. Rule Number 1—decide without redeciding. Make a decision and don't look back after you've made it. And Rule Number 2—don't decide until you've gotten past your doubts. Once you've made up your mind, decide and move on.

Decisions have their moment! Made too early the world they affect is spoiled. Great is the decider who knows the right time and does not allow himself to be badgered into bad timing.

One final aspect of decision making must be understood: team playing with the future.

Team Playing with the Future

Burt Nanus reminds us that good leaders are terminally clairvoyant. It is human, even exalted, to lead with far-sightedness. "The ability to think about the future is a distinctly human quality that sets us apart from all other species. This ability enables us to act not just in response to an actual physical stimulus, as all other animals do, but also to images of future worlds that exist only in the mind."[6]

Every leader knows the value of team playing, but in 2 Samuel 6:13, the issue is not just one of team playing for

COOK'S RULES FOR DECISION MAKING

RULE #1: DECIDE ONCE; DON'T REDECIDE

RULE #2: DECIDE ONLY AFTER YOU'RE THROUGH WITH ALL EVALUATION

the moment, but team playing for the future. God makes a marvelous point in this passage of Scripture: the way a leader's work survives may well depend upon those to whom any particular leader commits his vision. The constructing of the Rheims Cathedral was handed down from one generation to the next for hundreds of years. Would the impatience of most modern leaders permit this kind of commitment? We are always too anxious to finish our here-and-now work in the here-and-now.

Paul tells Timothy to entrust his teaching to reliable men who shall be able to teach others also (see 2 Tim. 2:2). Does he not indicate that straight thinking from one generation to another, in essence, team playing with the future?

So here in the life of David is another of those decisions to postpone. Postpone he does. Solomon, his son, will be his partner for decades he will never live to see. This youthful Prince Solomon will in time take his old father's frail hand. They will link their visions across a joint reign of eighty years. David will in God's good time permit his son to finish what he began.

Our future fears are completely groundless if we remember that God knows no future. Time is God's visible captive. He sees the front from the end and the end from the front. Our insecurities about our future are needless. Kellogg Albran wrote in *The Profit,* "I have seen the future. It is much like the present, only longer." And the unknown author of *The Cloud of Unknowing* wrote, "Man will not be able to excuse himself at the last judgment, saying to God, 'You overwhelmed me with the future when I was only capable of living in the present.' " Why will we not be able to excuse ourselves? Because our lives are called to serve the God who owns the future. We are not to play at our dreams alone. We are to commit these visions to those who come after us. We are always holding hands with the future.

Conclusion

If we intend to study how David and Solomon actually linked together across generations, we must see the dying David as he passes the baton of leadership to Solomon (1 Kings 1:32–35; 2:1–11). David knows this moment of passing, and understands that Solomon will live on. Death cannot eliminate the future. David dies on the threshold of his son's bright hopes. Optimism is a heritage.

John Maxwell tells of a conversation on a crowded elevator. One passenger seemed irritated by another's cheerfulness.

"What are you so happy about?" he snapped.

"Well, sir, I ain't never lived this day before!"[7]

Every great leader is a futurist. He always considers what today's decisions will mean in tomorrow's world. At age eighty-three, Frank Lloyd Wright was asked which of his works he would select as his most important. His answer was quick: "My next one!"[8] No leader is satisfied with yesterday's performance. The best is yet to take place.

I have always liked the story of the old Supreme Court Justice who was reading Plato. When asked, "Why are you reading Plato at your age?" he answered saucily, "Why, to improve my mind, of course." Everything worthwhile ends in the future.

The future can, of course, be scary. There is a mercy in our Heavenly Father that does not let us see very far down the road. Lee Iacocca beautifully expressed this view of the future: "It's a good thing God doesn't let you look a year or two into the future, or you might be surely tempted to shoot yourself. But He's a charitable Lord: He only lets you see one day at a time. When times get tough, there's no choice except to take a deep breath, carry on, and do the best you can."[9]

While God's mercy does not let us see very far down the road we must travel, He is also the wonderful God who lets us know the future is on the way. Thoughts of the future fuel every leader with zeal. True leaders do not glory in the past or present. The apostle Paul comments on what is probably the futuristic mind set of leaders: "But one thing I do: Forgetting what is behind and straining toward what is ahead, I press on toward the goal to win the prize for which God has called me heavenward in Christ Jesus" (Phil. 3:13–14, NIV).

In essence, this idea of the future comprises all that is brightest in human hope. Viktor Frankl, who spent the war years in a concentration camp, noticed that those who believed in tomorrow best survived the day. Those who believed that tomorrow would never come were those who could not survive: "The prisoner who had lost his faith in the future—his future—was doomed. With his loss of belief in the future, he also lost his spiritual hold; he let himself decline and become subject to mental and physical decay."[10] The future is glory! Indeed, the future is survival.

I have known many successful men and women. Without exception, all of them were healthy futurists with spirits of unbridled optimism. Unfortunately, pessimism often rules the day. John Kenneth Galbraith offers this haunting caveat: "Pessimism in our time is infinitely more respectable than optimism. The man who sees the decline in juvenile delinquency is a negligent, a fool and a foolish fellow. The man who foresees catastrophe has the gift of insight which will assure that he will become a famous radio commentator, the editor of *Time Magazine* or go to Congress."[11] Many successful people have adopted little slogans by whose help they ride out the rough times. Like Little Orphan Annie, they believe "the sun will come out tomorrow." Even under the heavy press of seeming failure, they cry, "When you walk through a storm hold your head up high." They are sloganeers of hope.

In the midst of crushing despair, the Christian leader also relies on the sufficiency of the Bible's great truth. In 1 John 3:2 we read, "Dear friends, now we are children of God, and what we will be has not yet been made known. But we know that when he appears, we shall be like him, for we shall see him as he is" (NIV). The motivation for believing in the future is hidden in God's continuing faithfulness. After all, "Jesus Christ is the same yesterday and today and forever" (Heb. 13:8, NIV).

Defining, Structuring, and Motivating

What is power? The "power of A over B," we are told,
"is equal to maximum force which A can induce on B
minus the maximum resisting force which B
can mobilize in the opposite direction."

James MacGregor Burns,
Leadership

Leaders must be able to spot roadblocks and clear them.

John White,
Excellence in Leadership

There have been meetings of only a moment
which have left impressions for life, for eternity.
No one can understand that mysterious thing
we call influence . . . yet . . . every one of us
continually exerts influence, either to heal, to bless,
to leave marks of beauty; or to wound,
to hurt, to poison, to stain other lives.

J. R. Miller,
The Building of Character

Letter 6

Dear Leader:

Do you remember that old hymn of invitation, "O Why Not Tonight?" Me too. Every time I heard that old song I would always say inside, Well, why not? *Remember "Give of Your Best to the Master"? Every time I heard that old song, something inside of me said,* OK, I will. *But that hymn, "Almost Persuaded!" Every time I heard that hymn, I was never quite persuaded . . . I almost was, but not quite.*

Well, the point is that most of us need a good kick in the pants to get us going from time to time. We need to be persuaded—totally motivated—not almost motivated.

Motivation for me is kind of like jump-starting a car. The other morning I went out, jumped in my car, thrust the key into the ignition, and turned it. Nothing happened. The starter didn't even buzz or click. The electrical system was rigor mortis—dead. Reminds me of a lot of Christians I know. Anyway, lucky for me I have two cars. One of them had an electrical system that was still quite alive, like some dynamic leaders I know. I always park my cars side by side at night. I have good, long jumper cables, and I used the living car to get the dead one going, so to speak. It always works.

I realize, Pastor, that you can only jump-start so many of us before you need a little juice yourself. Still, I gotta be motivated if I'm gonna get up and get goin'. So stay prayed up, 'cause most of us are gonna need a jump start on those cold, dead mornings of our discipleship. Just walk by us whistling, "Give of Your Best to the Master" or "Why Not Tonight?" Leave off that "Almost Persuaded." Also, nothing jump-starts me like great preaching. So preach passionately, like you really believe what you're saying. If you do, I will. I really want to be a dynamic Christian. I need to be. I ought to be. I will be if you're willing to jump-start me now and then.

—Your Follower

2 Samuel 8:1–18; 10:12

Every good leader must develop a structure for the vision. Without a structure or plan, visions can lose definition. The best plans and the most achievable goals are written down. Anthony Robbins cites a very commanding survey done by the Harvard Business School on its 1953 graduates. Only 3 percent of these graduates had written goals for their lives. Twenty years later, in 1973, the researchers went back and interviewed the surviving members of the 1953 graduating class. They discovered that the 3 percent with written specific goals were worth more in financial terms than the entire other 97 percent put together.[1] Such a survey teaches us that without structure and a plan there exists no form to direct the vision. The vision is then only a powerful locomotive without rails. When the vision waits for rails, motivation is impossible. Thus all concrete leadership begins with the leader's plan.

Leadership Is Proceeding with a Simple Plan

In 2 Samuel 8:1–3, David's course of military conquest followed a very simple plan; he subdued his enemies in an orderly campaign. One by one he encircled his own country with those he had conquered. He moved in a counterclockwise military operation that left Israel surrounded by subjugated people. David spent a lot of literal blood, sweat, and tears required in bringing all of this to pass, but the plan was simple.

Most good books on leadership say that it is important to keep your vision simple. Along with simplicity, two other issues are imperative in making any plan workable. The leader must prioritize which aspects of the plan are to be carried out first. But the second and most important aspect of bringing a vision to be demands that the plan be flexible. The most significant danger of simplicity is that it can cause us to commit the sin of inflexibility. Simple but supple is the way to make plans. If the plan has to be bent, then so be it, for the object of the leader's life is not to make plans but to achieve goals and bring visions to reality. "Don't wait to start your planning programs," says Joe Batten. "If you hold back until you are meticulously prepared in every detail to establish magnificent objectives, let's face it—you'll never get started. The important thing is to set your goals and get the planning machinery under way."[2]

Consider for a moment the structuring process you now have in place or need to have in place. If you have never done this, it would be good to write down your top three life priorities. Begin with the singularly most important goal of your life at the top of the list. Next, write down the second most important thing you would like to achieve. Continue on in descending order. Find a place to write them down where you must come across them from time to time. Maybe you want to write them in the front of your Day-timer, or on the flyleaf of your address file, or even in the back of your family Bible. Take your time in listing your life priorities. It is good not to scribble them hastily. Set them in your best hand. Write them down deliberately. As you do, pray about them. Make the writing of them a form of prayer. Consciously picture yourself offering this list of priorities as a sacrifice to God. See yourself in your mind's eye kneeling before God offering this neatly written list unto Him as the Magi offered gold to the Christ Child.

Indeed this should be the gold of your life: the treasure of all you want to be for Christ. In this pageant of the heart, you are giving unto Him the glorious possible. You know what the list will cost you in money and pain and years. But this splendid ritual of the soul is your private alleluia to the glory of His name. But you know that this is more than just a pageant of the heart. In this written, secluded drama of dreams, you make tangible the treasure of your life. This is a material plan physically written down in material ink on material paper. Your physical eye can see it. Your actual fingers will touch it. And here, in this deliberate intentional plan, real-world senses meet the inner aspirations of your heart. The goals themselves are

Four Steps for Arriving at Your

"WOE POINT"

1 CORINTHIANS 9:16

1 Write down your life priorities in descending order of importance.

2 Write them in a place where you must confront them often.

3 Write them in the form of a prayer to God.

4 Visualize their written form as an offering you lay on an altar.

written and as tangible as the desk where you inscribe them.

Even after praying long and hard, it may be difficult to write down the single most important thing you want to achieve in life. But do it in this way: Paul says in 1 Corinthians 9:16, "For though I preach the gospel, I have nothing to glory of: for necessity is laid upon me; yea, woe is unto me, if I preach not the gospel!" (KJV). In this verse of Scripture Paul is dealing with the basic goal of his life. In fact, he is stating his "Woe Point." Paul was saying, "Woe be unto me if I preach not the gospel." Try writing down your own life goal in terms of such a Woe Point. Write: "Woe be unto me if I do not _____." Now, where the blank is, write in your own "woe point" and finish in twenty-five words or less. This, of course, will give you a simply-written life plan.

But what of flexibility? Paul does not seem very flexible in stating his woe point, does he? Of course not. Woe points build simple, but inflexible goals. These are unalterable. What then alone builds flexibility in making simple life plans? The structure is one of implementation. How we put those plans into effect must remain fluid. If you consider Paul again in Acts 16:8ff, it is easy to tell he was determined to preach. His woe point was still in place, guiding him. What is not clear is where he would do it. Should he preach in Asia, Bithynia, or Greece? At this point the implementation of his life plans remains flexible. Always abandon unnecessary rigidity, for God can only direct the flexible.

Leadership Is Structuring for Stability

Plans should be exciting. They should be so exciting that they whip us into an emotional delirium of joy. There was a season in the life of American evangelicals when bus ministry was seen to be the wave of the future for church growth. Independent Baptists had made it work wonderfully and were growing large churches, ringed with fleets of yellow school busses. These busses were usually bought cheaply because the various school districts that sold them to the Baptists were generally elated to get rid of them. For the dying busses, the movement was redemptive, for many of these "Old Yellars" had been joyously rescued from salvage yards and pressed into the service of Jesus.

Our church began making plans to do the same. They were exciting plans. We, like thousands of other churches, would have our own fleet of redeemed, derelict busses. We would name our fleet (as so many churches did) after the four evangelists. We at first were so grandiose that we thought to acquire a fleet of twelve busses named after the minor prophets. Alas, however, we never progressed beyond Matthew and Mark. Our goal was to grow a church. Busses, however, did not work well in our upper-middle-class neighborhood. Like untrained puppies, they tended to spot elitist driveways with sludge, and the more upper-class children could not be induced to ride the aging yellow monsters. Bit by bit our wild enthusiasm cooled and soon we were altogether out of the bus business. Alas, poor Matthew and Mark went on to that great, golden salvage yard in the sky. Our plans had to be rewritten. What went wrong? We only had to set ourselves to re-structuring.

Structuring: Stabilize Achievements as You Achieve Them . . .

. . . so you never have to climb the same mountain twice. Steven Covey has referred to this kind of logic as the carpenter's rule: measure twice, cut once. Notice how David, according to 2 Samuel 8:6,14, did not just fight a war and collect booty. After he subjugated a nation, he garrisoned it; that is, he left soldiers there so that when he left, his influence remained. This made it unlikely that he would ever have to go back with a later conquest and reachieve what he had already accomplished.

Great leadership does not advance one ladder rung without determining that the part of the ladder just traversed is still secure. To keep from reinventing the wheel takes time. But reinventing it uses up life, not with progress, but with doubling back. As we pass each milestone in our career, it is important to secure that part of our lives so that repeating it will be unnecessary.

Saul preceded David. He fought as hard as David, and in many ways was as victorious as David in battle. If Saul was not as successful, it was because he never seemed to learn the knack of garrisoning what he had conquered. He kept fighting the Philistines over and over, often on the very same terrain.

I have watched a great many ministers across the years. The ones that seemed to succeed (and in some ways I hate using this word as the corporate world would; to succeed in Christ is to be faithful to our calling) were the ones who never backtracked and rarely changed churches. These pastors, it seemed to me, generally maintained a forward motion in ministry. Others, like Saul, from year to year fought the same old angry Philistines. Sadly, as in the case of Saul, the Philistines often won the last battle. The pastor, broken in health with little or no retirement, lived out his final days in our old folks home. He who had given so much wound up abandoned. Those preachers' battles are great, and our latter-life insecurities can leave us on the ropes. How much pain we might avoid if, like David, we would fight the Philistines only once, then garrison Philistia, and then move on to an orderly and stabilized career.

Pastors often lead compassionate lives, caring about all who are in need. They drift, however, between needy parishioners who get their full attention. But in the last analysis, these compassionate drifters never organize their own life priorities. They tend ecclesiastical machines with no written goals that lead them to measurable and secure futures.

Stabilizing: Setting Reasonable Intermediate Goals

Since "woe points" are rarely reached in giant steps, it is very important to break down the long-range goals of our lives into intermediate steps. What rarely gets noticed in the conquests of David was that the war to establish his empire was gained by little battles. In 1966 I had the desire to plant a large, growing Baptist church somewhere beyond the Mason-Dixon line. I wanted this church to be at least five hundred miles north of the buckle of the Bible Belt. Shortly after going to Omaha, I realized that this could not be done by a single strategy. I mapped out several intermediate steps, like (1) gathering a formative congregation, (2) becoming financially self-sufficient, (3) organizing the church into a working, functioning body, (4) buying a piece of ground in West Omaha, and (5) raising capital funds to build with. Only by setting such intermediate goals could I arrive at my overall, long-term goal.

What I earlier said about making flexible plans proved all-important. I was not able to see how rapidly, in some ways, our aggressively growing church would gobble its way through the temporary goals I had set. Having arrived faster at planting the church than I thought we might, I had to go back to the drawing board in the middle eighties and "re-flexibilize" my earlier plans. These "flexibilized" plans included beginning an area-wide telecast, relocating the church to a new and more roomy campus, and finally, building a multi-million dollar complex to continue seeing the church grow. In the process of stabilizing my long-term goals, I had to restructure with intermediate goals. As in the case of the overall life plan I discussed earlier, I think it is also good to write down our own intermediate goals to these plans. The amended plans must themselves be left open to amendment. Such constantly amended plans cannot become a final script of one's life pageant, but are most necessary as we structure for stability.

The Consequences Beyond

There is an old story that tells of a town dog, an unkept stray, that had a habit of chasing trains. One of the local spit-and-whittlers observed the old dog chase the 5:35

Frisco away from the station. He was heard to remark, "I wonder what that old dog'd do if he caught that thing?"

The story points up the sin of hunting without ammunition. Within the context of any denomination we must buy into certain expected values. In the Baptist denomination it is most important to talk about "personal evangelism." Even those who never do it must pay it some lip service just to keep their self-respect. Naturally, therefore, we all talk the game. This particular game defines who we are.

It is like those pheasant hunts in which I used to participate. On the day that the game was short, some of our crew would walk all day long dressed in hunter's khaki, with their shotguns at a forty-five-degree tilt across their chests. I couldn't help but wonder if their guns were really loaded. They looked like hunters, dressed like hunters, talked like hunters. During our field breaks they would drink coffee in the frosty foliage and tell old hunter's tales. But if there is no ammunition in the gun, it may be said that they only professed while they lived in unbelief.

The greatest sin of appearing to be a leader is going out to do battle with no real commitment to the war. Such warriors have never made a decision about what they would do with success if they bagged it. The dream that David had, like all good dreams, pictured not just his attaining of the goal but what David would look like and how he would live once his dream was complete. "Meaningful, stimulating goals must be preceded and nourished by a dream. This gives goals a 'being' flavor rather than a self-defeating focus on activities or doing. Having a dream also means that goals will be focused on aspirations beyond your immediate knowledge and skill level, thus providing stretch. . . . Goals should be achievable and attainable in order to satisfy clearly charted expectations. It is important, however, that your overall dream provide a continuous need to improve and grow."[3] Even more important than his own finished image, David dreamed what the nation would look like when they were strong enough to live with peace on every side.

The visions of our finished plan must include our certainty about what we are going to do with our dreams once they come true. There are few who ever live out their dream and never lose faith in their coming success.

Back to the pheasant hunt for a moment; the first time I ever went, I went with an eager beaver who felt that the season had opened too early that October. He felt we should take a tub of ice so we could field dress the birds we bagged and ice them down. He felt that the unusually warm weather would cause the many birds that we shot early in the day to spoil if they were not properly iced. Thus we sallied off, loaded with ammunition and a tub of ice to refrigerate all the birds we would kill that day. We walked nearly across the state of Nebraska, and for some particular reason saw only a few birds (which were, of course, too far out of range to shoot). We ended up not killing a single bird. At dusk we mocked our friend, making fun of the tub of ice that he insisted that we bring. Still, deep down in our critical hearts, we liked being with a man who planned for the future. He was setting goals for all of us. And all of us knew that a tub of unused ice is far superior to a bag of rotting birds.

The Sin of Capriciously Changing Life Plans

I speak a lot to college students. Often those messages turn to the issue of what they are going to do with their lives. One doctrine I always preach to them is: "Young men and women, you can *be* anything you want to be. You can *achieve* anything you want to achieve. All you have to do is start early on your dreams and never change your mind." Nearly every time I see someone who has failed to achieve what they once termed success, one of two issues is usually at fault. They may have started too late in life to make it all happen, or they may have started early enough on their career but kept changing their minds. Roaming from career to career, they, at last, had not enough of life left to accomplish anything.

Nothing is so counterproductive as the constant changing of life directions. Sound dreams are victimized by the capricious winds of change. James Beall counsels us: "The leader/influencer cannot be a person who follows every 'charismatic fad.' He must be a man who has a clear philosophy of life, precise and attainable goals, and walks—not runs—toward the declared target."[4] Not only is career-chasing befuddling to the person doing it, but it is awfully hard on family and friends. Such pastors condemn churches to live without a "why." When a pastor constantly changes plans, churches vibrate but never move. I once had a pastor friend who served in a different denomination. He was motivated to grow a church. His inspiration came from a number of different mega-church motivators. He decided that, like Bob Schuller, he would build a drive-in church in Omaha. Then I reminded him that, unlike California (where you can go to a drive-in church all year round), our state had severe weather. Our Nebraska February could so fog up the inside of a windshield you wouldn't be able to see an open-air preacher. Further, the preacher would have to preach in a parka and ski mask to deliver the word of God. Besides, open-air parishioners would find their fingers frostbitten, just reaching out to get the window speakers. I suggested that he should also have a healing ministry just to take care of the frostbite. He confessed that he was not particularly good at faith healing and didn't want to preach in a ski mask. So, gradually, with better judgment he gave up his plans for an open-air church.

Still, there were other role models he followed. He felt compelled to mimic other heroes. It was not long before his admiration for John MacArthur lured him to use an overhead projector as he launched his new oral exegesis sermon style. His church was quite liturgical and so the exegetical style never fit very well. Besides, the bottom of the sermon outlines would often project off into the faces of choir members who objected to Greek verb roots shining in their eyes. So, in time, he decided to be a little more like Bill Hybels and have a trap set and a brass combo. His Jesus-Thou-Joy choir director, however, very much objected to this new skotty-wotty-doo-doo-doo worship style.

His story is longer than this chapter needs to tell. Still I couldn't help but wonder what his bewildered people must have thought as he led them from spasm to spasm. He was always so intrigued by someone else's model for church growth that he never seemed to come up with any of his own. When he had blazed through his best ideas, the Lord led him to another congregation. Amid the cheers of his tired congregation, he left the city. I have since lost track of him, but I have no doubt he has taken his "trying" ministry somewhere else. There he is still trying new ideas while trying the patience of those he leads.

Constant caprice in our life plans can bring early closure both to our lives and to our authenticity. Leadership should never be predictable. Further, it should always be flexible, but spastic is another thing!

Leadership Is Being Able Both to Motivate and Administrate

There can be little doubt that motivation is learning the balance between praise and reprimand. In his book *The One Minute Manager,* Ken Blanchard lists his three secrets of one-minute management: "GOALS start performance in the right direction. PRAISINGS foster improvement in the development level of individuals. REPRIMANDS stop poor performance."[5]

Motivating generally takes a lot more praising than reprimand. However, for every one reprimand we ought to offer a score of praisings. Positive reinforcement builds positive, aggressive team members. Reprimands build tentative, cautious players.

Blanchard's Three Indispensable

AXIOMS
OF
MANAGEMENT

GOALS
Keep Things Moving

PRAISINGS
Foster Development

REPRIMANDS
Stop Poor Performance

Not much needs to be said about this now. We will deal with it thoroughly in another chapter. However, in 2 Samuel 8:15 there is a clear indication that David could both administrate as well as motivate. How happy is the church where this is so. Being moved to accomplish some great goal is an elixir that intoxicates. But once we arrive there, often the last meaningful thing the leader says is, "Well, folks, here we are!" We look around and, sure enough, we are "there." At first we reason that it is okay to be "there," because indeed everybody has to be somewhere. But before long, we begin to realize that being there is not enough. We must have some further word to tell us why we are there, what it means to be there, and above all what we're to do next.

Compliments will goad a team to its corporate goal. But the achievement celebration only causes them to look forward to the next pinnacle of accomplishment. All achievement always points to this key motivating truth: being there is never as important as getting there.

In Shaw's marvelous play *Pygmalion,* Eliza Doolittle was at first delighted that Henry Higgins would work so hard to make a lady out of her. She is later chagrined that once she has become a lady, Higgins has no further plans for her. I have often wondered why so many pastors barely survive a building program. Is it that they mistakenly thought that reaching this one plateau was all they were supposed to do? Now that they are there, all too quickly the people begin asking, "What happens next?" It is when they shrug their shoulders in uncertainty that the deacons begin to suspect the pastor is out of leadership goals.

Such a mistaken notion of leadership fosters the lie, "Getting there is more important than being there!" Such short-sighted leadership convinces people to follow their conquistador, plant the flag, and occupy the future. But once the flag goes down, the obligation of answering why the church exists is awesome. It is like a group of actors lamenting, "Now that the theater is built, does anybody have a play we can perform?" Great leaders never allow finales. They always promise that the future is still there and it is still a place of hope. Great leaders always say, "This show, while I lead, will always be in process. It will never be finished. Now that we stand on this plateau, I would like you to lift up your eyes to the next. We are here, it is true. But we were never called of God to be here. Rather there. See? Over there? Yes, there lies our destiny! Do not celebrate overly on this small pinnacle. The mountain we are sent to conquer is yet to be climbed and we must begin at once. I've only given you this brief plateau to enable you to see the next."

Leadership Is Motivating by Example

There are all kinds of theories about how to lead. I think the best of all of them call for role modeling. Albert Schweitzer said that leadership is example. Edmund Burke wrote long ago, "Example is the school of mankind, and he will learn at no other." Tom Peters wrote the following: "People in organizations are all boss-watchers, especially when external conditions are ambiguous. For better or for worse, what you spend your time on (not what you sermonize about) will become the organization's preoccupation."[6] David makes a wonderful statement in 2 Samuel 10:12: "Be of good courage, and let us play the men for our people" (KJV). The best leadership models the how-to's spoken in every motivational speech.

I have long believed that the word *pastor* or *shepherd* is the best title for a church leader. The idea of shepherding implies that the leader is always out in front (for sheep are never driven) showing the sheep which way to go. One reads so much in these days of the urban society that the word *shepherd* is out of mode—belonging to an earlier agrarian world, some say. However, I rarely hear them suggest a synonym for pastor that I am willing to trade for this noble designation. Many times the word *rancher,* the new mega-church word for leadership, is suggested as a better choice. But *rancher* somehow dilutes the shepherd metaphor that Jesus used of Himself.

For church administration, the model of player and coach comes to mind. This model of leadership works best.

Why? Because the team needs to know how to get the job done, and they lack know-how and often the courage to get started. The inspiring figure of a pastor-administrator actually showing the sheep how to do it means much.

Ken Blanchard says that the successful leader will achieve by two leadership behaviors: directive behavior and supportive behavior. Directive behavior involves "clearly telling people what to do, how to do it, where to do it, and when to do it, and then closely supervising their performance." Supportive behavior, on other hand, involves "listening to people, providing support and encouragement for their efforts, and then facilitating their involvement in problem-solving and decision-making."[7]

The concept came home quite clearly to me when I first began to teach personal evangelism to the people of our congregation. I fully believe that pastors cannot inspire laymen to leap over their fear of the subject while the minister's own fear keeps him or her locked inside. There is no doubt about it: personal evangelism is the fearsome work of the church. Within the fellowship, we can achieve almost any other kind of church service with seminars and instruction manuals. Praying, teaching a Bible class, going to the hospital—all these include elements of fear. But these fears are more easily transcended than the fear of witnessing. When a church visitor, who has gone out to a home for the express purpose of "sharing Christ" knocks on a door, the worst of all possible fears begins to occupy that life.

Consider the paranoia that operates on a church evangelism call. Two people have gone to present Christ. They arrive at a suburban home they hope to evangelize. They lay a trembling finger on the doorbell—that pearlized, spongy button that rings somewhere on the other side of a wall. There, where the door chimes sound, is a family huddled together. This fearful family, hearing the doorbell ring, looks outside and notices that those on the doorstep look like church people. They falteringly go to the door, desperately wishing the church visitors were at someone

Two Winning Behaviors of
THE LEADERSHIP MYSTIQUE

DIRECTIVE

Clearly Spelling
Out Individual
Expectations

Listening to
Encourage,
Facilitate, and
Build Decisiveness

SUPPORTIVE

else's house. Meanwhile, there on the front step, the church visitors also quail in terror, desperately praying that no one is home. Thus, both the visitors and the visitees meet each other in abject terror. The door swings open and the host says, "Yes, how may I help you?" Fears and suspicions fly! The church visitors wish they would have simply said, "Glory be to God, it's some wonderful people from the church! Oh, please, saints of God, I've been trying so hard to find Christ. I beg of you, tell me, what must I do to be saved?" But the host is really saying, "Oh, God, help me to remember something godly that I can say. Where is my confirmation certificate now that I need it? You can always ward off an army of Baptist soul winners with one old yellow, Episcopal certificate."

Such terrible terror is best assuaged when the pastor leads such fearful sheep to face their fears. Role modeling, said David, is "playing the man for the people" (2 Sam. 10:12). This kind of role modeling is never easy. The *modeler* never finds it any easier than the *learner*. Still, the point is that until the leader confronts his or her fears, the people will not confront theirs.

Conclusion

Defining, structuring, and motivating may all three resolve themselves in this most basic issue of role modeling. The world is looking for a leader who has not only been there, but even as he leads, is going there. The best leaders have never merely pointed the way. They have said, "C'mon, let's go!"

Once when I was visiting in Denmark, I became lost in Copenhagen. I was walking along, reading a map, trying to make it yield up its cryptic information. It wouldn't serve. At length I was so frustrated, I asked a young bicyclist if he could point me to such and such a street. At first he pointed, explaining the way to me in Danish. When he saw that my ignorance of maps was further complicated by our language barrier, he must have said something like, "Follow me!" I did. And he gave me a wonderful gift in this simple act of friendship. Leaders who lead the way will always out-succeed leaders who only point the way. You cannot lead an army by bringing up the rear.

So go ahead, define your leadership. Structure your organization. Motivate all who follow for the entire journey. And above all, remember this: When Jesus wanted to

The Three Piers of
C'MON-LET'S-GO LEADERSHIP

DEFINING

STRUCTURING

MOTIVATING

train some old fishers in a new kind of angling, He cried in Matthew 4:19, "Follow me, and I will make you fishers of men!" (KJV). And so they followed the model. Within a couple of decades they had snagged the Roman Empire in their nets.

The Politics of Grace
and
the Abuse of Power

Assumption of personal authority,
marked self-confidence and political skill,
the diminution of legislative and party opposition,
personal and dramatic links with the people,
the exploitation of emergency powers—
these are the qualities of executive leadership.

James MacGregor Burns,
Leadership

The power to persuade is the power to bargain.

Richard Neustadt,
Presidential Power

Someone says:
"The only thing that walks back
from the tomb with the mourners
and refuses to be buried, is the character."
This is true.
What a man is, survives him.
It never can be buried.

J. R. Miller,
The Building of Character

Letter 7

Dear Leader:

I can't understand why everybody gets so on edge when they hear the word politics. *Politics is nothing more than the benefits one enjoys as a result of his or her relationships. When people say, for instance, that they won't put up with politics in the church, what they generally mean is that they don't like seeing people enjoying the benefits of a system from which they are excluded. The word* clique *similarly refers to small groups that offer warm, political blessings for all who belong to them. The only ones who ever complain about church cliques are those who feel they don't belong to one.*

If you look at it right, politics is nothing more than the science of involvement. The key to a happy church, therefore, is making sure that it centers around an endless chain of involvements, where everybody gives and receives from their relationships. No one likes to live in a community that they feel really isn't theirs. Remember Cinderella, that long-ago victim of community exclusion? All she wanted was a little music and a chance to meet a few nice people, maybe even a prince. I guess we all know how the story really went. Until her fairy godmother showed up, I'll bet she went around saying things like, "Everything's a matter of politics over at the castle. As soon as I get the chance I'm blowin' this joint. This isn't my community. I hate castle politics."

But one "bibbity bobbity boo" later, there she is dancing with the prince. Ultimately she winds up princess. After that you never once hear her complain. She was suddenly part of the "in crowd." After that, she played a lot of golf and bridge with some pretty important people. She was in the society column a lot too.

Once she was on the inside, it completely escaped her attention that there were still a lot of small critics of castle politics. They were the ones still sleeping in fireplaces and waiting for their own fairy godmother and a little of that bibbity-bobbity-boo sociology that's such a windfall when you can't get invited to the galas at the center of palace life.

I don't want to complain, Pastor, but some of your church members are like Cindy's stepsisters. You know how I hate church politics while I am still waiting my turn to dance. You'd better get some political system going that will make a place for me. I would never join a church so full of cliques unless, of course, I'm in one.

—Your Follower

2 Samuel 9:1–13

Politics is often a word of contempt for people in the church. Church politics somehow seem more ungodly than civil politics. "We must keep politics out of the church," say the offended.

Mark this!

In every organization, including the church, the leader must be somewhat of a politician. He or she must learn how to motivate various people by making commitments, side deals, complimenting, remonstrating, and bargaining in order to get things done. In 2 Samuel 9, David demonstrated the political overtones of his leadership. Do not think David unspiritual for behaving as he does toward Mephibosheth. The truth is, he is being especially effective.

I remember being terribly incensed some years ago when a friend of mine suggested that every successful pastor was a politician. I determined that even if he spoke the truth, I would rather not succeed than use politics in any aspect of my ministry. I actually held some resentment toward him until I later read a similar statement in a book by a pastor-writer whom I had always admired. At that time I tried to convince myself that I was living free of the whole issue. But in later moments of honest thought, I realized that politics need not be a dirty word when used in the context of ministry.

Our distaste for church politics swelters in the aftermath of national scandals like Watergate and those of cable television evangelists. The truth of the matter is, *politics* isn't always a dirty word; it's the means using our sphere of interpersonal relationships in ways that enable us to accomplish our goals. *Politics* is defined in the dictionary as the "art and science of government . . . the art of influencing policy or winning control." There's a secondary meaning of *politics* that emphasizes competition between groups or individuals for power and leadership.

Of course, the very suggestion that pastors or churches ought to be locked in egoistic power struggles is unworthy of the cross of Christ. But let us remember that the word *politics* derives from the same term as the words polity and polite. *Polity* is the word for cooperation in and understanding within the community. *Polite* refers to any action that is marked by courtesy, consideration, or correct social usage.

I would like us to focus on the use of the word *politics* as it regards courtesy and correct social usage. Jesus certainly did not encourage power struggles in the church. He did say that kindness and courtesy were to be the laws of His kingdom. He said that the Christian was to be wise, knowing his world, but harmless as far as the desire for power or control was concerned (see Matt. 10:16). He even went so far as to compliment an unjust steward by saying that the children of this world are wiser in their generation than the children of light (see Luke 16:8). Is Jesus condoning a "Watergate" in the church? Of course not! But He is saying the kind of diplomacy and courtesy employed in the world might be of benefit in the kingdom of God.

Practically, this means you are not free as a Christian to compete with selfish power in the church. Sadly, there are many who have made the church a forum for political abuse. Warren Bennis speaks for churches as well as secular society when he says that too often we don't want leaders anymore; we want conspirators.[1] It isn't just the conspirators that Christians admire; they also admire superstar believers. We evangelicals often elevate our superstars to idol status. We gape at them and hunger for their autographs. Why? Because they are great leaders? No! Because they give us a feeling of touching greatness with none of the demands that great leaders endure. We elevate them to marquis status because they flatter us in allowing us to know them while they require nothing of us. We sometimes create non-content neurotics by our adulation, knowing that it is a lot easier to live with stars than leaders.[2]

Leaders can make us feel uncomfortable for our small commitments. Christians in many cases avoid their kingdom responsibilities and snuggle into an affirming and undemanding community. Christians should seek to promote God's kingdom in the hearts of men and to establish the church of Jesus. If by courtesy, deference, or kindness you cause enemies to love each other or the power-prone to submit to Christ, then politics is good. The key to the whole issue is this: Are you using deference, courtesy, and public relations to get others to grant you power, or are you using these things to create a wider sphere of influence for God?

It is wise to remember that Jesus was victimized by civil politics at His trial. Although He had all power, He succumbed to the political machinery of the Romans, Pharisees, Sadducees, and Zealots. His life was crushed. Much harm is done in the church because we forget the corrupting nature of power. It is easy to want to control others for our own advantage. We easily degenerate to tit-for-tat administration. We quickly learn the spiteful art of battling politics with politics. The cross always reminds us that we are not here to control others in the interests of building our own empires.

Peter Koestenbaum recognized that the best use of power contains at least one element of altruism. "Leadership is the use of power. But power, to be ethical, must never be abused. To ensure that, one rule cannot be broken: Power is to be used only for the benefit of others, never for yourself. That is the essential generosity and self-sacrifice of the leader."[3] Remember, self-sacrifice, like that Paul charges in Galatians 2:20, is not only the key to holiness, it is the door to Christian leadership.

In 2 Samuel, David of Israel used his old friendship with Jonathan to promote goodwill between warring political camps. David used deference and courtesy in a splendid way. He befriended Mephibosheth, Jonathan's crippled son. The result of his kindness to Jonathan's son produced a new harmony and better relationships in Israel. With this kindness, David practiced the politics of grace.

The politics of grace is built upon an understanding that wherever human beings gather they form a community of need. The politics of grace explains their attractions. The grace that lies at the center of the Christian community should be marked with a special kind of politics. This politic of relationships should be fueled by a New Testament ethic.

Themes That Empower
CHRISTIAN LEADERSHIP

✔ **Make People Feel Significant**

✔ **Teach All That Learning and Competence Matter**

✔ **Inspire Community**

✔ **Incite Vision**

Warren Bennis gives to my whole view of leadership four themes that should empower Christian leadership. First, people must feel significant. Second, learning and competence matter. This is important in Christian leadership, for one sometimes gets the feeling that Christians feel that merely the adjective *Christian* makes every value superior. How wrong! Christian leadership must also touch these sound bases of competence and learning. Incompetence and ignorance cannot sanctify what is shoddy and unstructured, even if it wears the word *Christian*. Third, people are and must be part of a community. Hopefully this community endows its constituents with largesse. Sometimes the Christian community cannot produce great leaders, because it builds only little souls nourished on stingy dogma and legalisms. Fourth, vision should make work exciting. Growing churches may be hard work but its people never complain. Excitement sanctifies work.[4]

The Politics of Leadership

Moderating Conflict

In 2 Samuel 2–4, David and his supporters killed all of the house of Saul to keep any claimants to that dynasty from rising in revolt. Doubtless there were deep grudges throughout the kingdom because of this purge. In 2 Samuel 9:1, we see David looking for new ways to bring those diehards, still loyal to the house of Saul, into orbit with his own goals.

Did David do anything illicit in looking for political answers to resolve this quarrel between the two families? No. Unfortunately, his blood-drenched military purge against Saul's clan had resolved the matter. However, his bloody constraint was succeeded by the politics of grace.

I have never known a pastor who did not seek to make decisions that would make the greatest number of people happy. In no church is it always possible to make everybody happy. But harmony must prevail at a reasonable level to keep the church moving ahead.

Gaining Support

Patronage refers to the use of special-interest actions to gain support. Jesus' final words in the parable of the dishonest steward are, "Use worldly wealth to gain friends for yourselves" (Luke 16:9, NIV). Jesus' statement is almost the dictionary definition of *patronage*. Does Jesus' statement imply that it is good to use patronage to provide people with future security? In certain instances Jesus seemed to say it is acceptable. Jesus had another parable in which He endorsed the right to spend money in political ways that we might be received into eternal habitations (Luke 16:10).

In what ways did David exercise good leadership in his patronage of Mephibosheth (2 Sam. 9:3–7)? In the kindness that he showed, was he only buttering him up to collect patronage? With so many people in the house of Mephibosheth and Ziba, it must have taken quite a bit of the king's resources to feed and clothe them. A real leader can sometimes see, however, that money must be spent to change discord into harmony.

All of us can remember a time when we saw our pastor (or other church leaders) take special-interest action to bring a sense of harmony and peace to the whole church. The actions of a good pastor would harmonize such special-interest action with the beatitude, "Blessed are the peacemakers" (Matt. 5:9, NIV). Every notable leader, from Abraham to the present time, has tried to work out political compromises that would harmonize hostilities without war.

The key issue is that in playing politics, a leader does not begin to use power abusively. It is dehumanizing—even ungodly—to exercise abusive power over others. Rollo May writes, "No human being can stand the perpetually numbing experience of his own powerlessness."[5] The problem is that no matter how we struggle to be free of being abusive, we are all tempted to want to control others. One gets the feeling in watching so many abusers of power that this desire to be king of the world is no laughing matter. So many evangelical power magnets seem possessed of an ungodly desire to build video empires at any cost. It is hard to tell how far they want to go with this, but they develop movements that have almost cult-like status.

Myron C. Madden warned us that seemingly God-filled people may, in reality, be agents of evil. "Evil, which is at the core of all temptations, seems to reside near the centers of power. That power may be political, religious, financial, intellectual or social, and it can change channels without high conversion costs."[6] Warren Bennis, like Madden, agrees about the dangers of evil always inherent in such cult-like leaders. He says that when cults develop around leaders, they get a God-complex, believing themselves infallible. Further, says Bennis, such idolatry of leadership can turn those who do the idolizing into drones who are so content to worship a corporate idol they no longer develop their own creative powers.[7]

How Christianity longs for a new Elijah to come and state the plan of God without using his proclamations to become rich.

The path to abusive power is easily traceable. It begins simply in our need for appreciation. From there the path winds upward to self-esteem, which—when it takes itself too seriously—moves toward arrogance. Arrogance often disparages others and leads to abusive power.

The current culture has made power a god. Its sole religious quest is how to achieve this power. The new heroes of culture are not the creative achievers but merely the powerful. Warren Bennis describes Americans well. He says that we have changed heroes. We used to admire people who achieved in theater or sports or human service. Now, however, we are in a mindset that admires tycoons, entrepreneurs, and CEOs. We no longer have heroes who do things, only heroes who occupy spotlights of wealth and visibility. We show we are infatuated with the rich and famous.[8] I wish I could say the church was free of these delusions, but alas, there seems to be an admiration of America's "religious names," not for what they believe or how they minister, but almost totally for the strength of their control or the size of their church or media empires.

How far we have gone since people like Carey or Judson were icons of evangelical respect!

The roots of abusive power are often found in the very men and women who were once victimized by power. For this reason Rollo May, in his book *Power and Innocence*, says that it is not always power that corrupts; indeed, powerlessness may be the corrupter. Powerlessness may be a prison for the unconquered spirit—a prison from which cellmates dream of being free and, once free, create the same abusive cells of powerlessness in which they force others to live.

Sigmund Freud noticed that most boys had psychological vendettas against their fathers. In early life these vendettas can lead them to begin vying with their fathers for power. Such vendettas produce powerful men who wield great, and sometimes abusive, power. James MacGregor Burns, in his Pulitzer Prize-winning book *Leadership*, says that Adolph Hitler is rumored to have been born with an undescended testicle. Such a child in a male-oriented world may struggle to achieve power in order to compensate for his deformity.[9]

The shift in those whom secular America lionizes is lamentable. Warren Bennis says that eighteenth-century America was famous for its geniuses, nineteenth-century America for its adventurers and creative discoverers. But what of twentieth-century America? Alas, we are defined only by our drudges, bureaucrats, and corporate machine tenders.[10] Is it possible that in the world of religion we must be labeled with the same spurious admiration? Do our young pastors too much admire the spiritual giants or the new video icons of power? Our own spiritual deformity may be so twisted as to make Mephibosheth look like a marathon titlist.

When examining David's role in history, it is futile to speak of his character as the result of an oppressive father or a physical deformity. The truth is, God placed David in a leadership role in order to forge a disorganized, tribal government into a nation. David clearly was not crushed by feelings of powerlessness, but he must have had such feelings from time to time.

Any condition of powerlessness, such as not being esteemed in childhood, may cause a person to strive extra hard to become an influential adult. Comedian Rodney Dangerfield has popularized the idea of how the lack of our esteem can cripple us. "I don't get no respect," he laments for everyone who feels the impact of powerlessness.

Did David ever feel that he "got no respect?" In the case of David's anointing (see 1 Sam. 16), his father Jesse appeared to esteem him least of all his sons. David's menial job of shepherding suggested—if only by reason of his youth—that he was not esteemed competent to go to war. If so, David's powerlessness may have become a springboard into the center of attention and national leadership.

We cannot assume that David tried to show the world that he "got no respect" and thus became a political super-achiever. Nor did David exhibit after his rise to the throne very many abuses of power. The growth of personal authority can be a platform for effective leadership, but it can also be the threshold of exploitation and power abuse. Most of David's life was marked by effective leadership, but in 2 Samuel 11 we see power abuse.

Leaders whom James MacGregor Burns would call "moral leaders" are those whose motivation is to produce changes in the world that will be of real value to both the leader and those he leads.[11] However, abusive power fails to see the followers and makes decisions in which the welfare of others is not a real concern. In such a "pro-me" use of others, the universe becomes a "you-niverse" in which others exist solely to supply the advance of the power abuser.

I suspect that most power-mad leaders never define themselves that way. Their erosion to the abusive use of power was so gradual that they may not have seen it. On their way up the ladder of control, they may well have served those they led; they were moral leaders. But once they gained the pinnacle of control, the power they had once been willing to share became their sole pursuit.

The pinnacle of position that power-mad leaders occupy often causes people around them to admire, and even envy, them. Admiration often feeds our cancerous self-esteem until we, in Muhammed Ali fashion, can say with little embarrassment that we really are the greatest! Arrogance, when well fed, begins to believe that the world owes it whatever it can seize.

This was apparently David's philosophy in 2 Samuel 11. How did it develop? We cannot know exactly when and where David's sinful abuse of power began. We can see that by 2 Samuel 11 the king's heart had turned from servant leadership toward scandalous power. Servant leadership is that all-important checkpoint that bridles demonic power. Max DePree said: "The first responsibility of a leader is to define reality, the last is to say 'thank you.' In between the two, the leader must become a servant and a debtor. That sums up the progress of an artful leader."[12]

As long as we follow Christ, we are safe! It is impossible to live out Christian servanthood and wield the mace of abusive power. He who tries to rule from the throne of Christ is a usurper, and not a servant. David learned this truth as a consequence of his evil deeds. In Psalm 51 we see that David had learned the beauty of the words that close the Lord's Prayer: "Thine is the kingdom and the power" (Matt. 6:13, KJV).

We are servants as long as we remember what Jesus said to Pilate: "You would have no power over me if it were not given to you from above" (John 19:11, NIV). We need to repeat this truth in every area of leadership to ensure that we truly are servant leaders.

FIVE EVIDENCES OF POWER ABUSE

 Giving up those disciplines we still demand of underlings.

 Believing that others owe us whatever use we can make of them.

 Trying to fix things up rather than make things right.

 Closing our minds to every suggestion that we ourselves could be out of line.

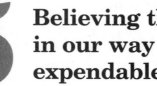 Believing that people in our way are expendable.

Power Abuse Evidence #1:
Giving Up Those Disciplines
We Demand of "Underlings"

"At the time when kings go off to war," David stayed home
(2 Sam. 11:1, NIV). No reason is offered for his failure to go
with the army. He did not seem to be ill or incapacitated.
War is dangerous, but David was no coward. War is hard,
but David had always thrived on what was difficult. Why
didn't David go to war? It appears as though he had excused
himself from war solely on the basis that he was king and
could do as he wished. His self-excusing reason may have
been, "Even though it is customary, I owe this to me." We
have already said that power abuse is rooted in selfishness.
David, as some see it, killed Uriah to take his wife. David
must have viewed dying as the duty of underlings while he
had the right to enjoy the more exalted status of being king!
It is a fault of power abusers that they come to overvalue
their own lives as they devalue others. Some men, they feel,
are created *more equal* than others. Is such a degenerative
view of human dignity common in all power abuse?

Power Abuse Evidence #2:
Believing That Others Owe Me
Whatever Use I Can Make of Them

In 2 Samuel 11:2–3, Bathsheba and her husband became
objects for David's personal use. Power abuse is always
characterized by the use of people. Some pastors and religious workers have found ladders to their own personal
success right within church. They rise to power using those
they were called to serve. Even as they use others, they
falsely quote Philippians 2, which speaks of the Christ who
humbled Himself and became nothing. They do not always
realize what they are doing. When confronted with their
abuse, they deny it. They wish for the more humbling
image of themselves that they prefer. Is it possible that
David continued writing psalms while using Bathsheba
and plotting her husband's death? Is it possible that he

was even faithful in his attendance at temple worship during this season of power abuse?

Years ago I had a friend whose life I longed to emulate. She seemed to have such a successful walk with Christ. More than anything, she seemed to long for Christlikeness. Just when I had nearly canonized her as a saint, she snapped her fingers, wrote her family off, and acknowledged her adulterous affairs with several men. She had grown so powerful in her company that she seemed to feel that her wealth and influence gave her a right to live any way she chose.

Power Abuse Evidence #3:
Trying to Fix Things Up
Rather Than Make Things Right

This evidence of power abuse shows the art of manipulating circumstances without moral conscience. David's sin in 2 Samuel 11:6 was that he didn't start to mend his ways by confessing his sin. Instead, he engineered the course of his life to a favorable end. It allowed him to retain his kingly image rather than face the hard moral and spiritual work of getting right with God.

So often in life we find ourselves making a mess of our circumstances. Yet we often think in terms of how to fix things up rather than to make things right. This tendency is common with power abusers. David ultimately gets things right with God, but his first attempt was to fix things up. It usually doesn't occur to us to ask God to make things right while we are trying to fix things. Fixing mess-ups falls short of being mended by the atoning work of Christ.

Power Abuse Evidence #4:
Closing My Mind to Every Suggestion
That I Could Be Out of God's Will

If King David had been sensitive to walking with God, he would have heard Uriah's counsel as a rebuke; the men of Israel were dying in the field and therefore Uriah would not live at home in selfish ease (2 Sam. 11:11). Are we so involved in selfish indulgence that we are blind to the sign-posts that God puts in our way to call us to Himself? How we need to keep our eyes open to the lessons God sends our way. Second Samuel 11:11 is evidence that power blinds us to God's rebuke. Other incidents in David's story allow us to see that God had to nudge David toward repentance. How often like David we pursue pleasure while others die in pain or live under great hardship. How often the American church lives it up while Christian brothers in other cultures are dying in need. Even if we do not in such moments see ourselves as indulgent, we are called the "ugly Americans" or even the "ugly Christians" because we are blind to our own narcissism and power hungry egoism.

Power Abuse Evidence #5:
Believing That People in
My Way Are Expendable

In 2 Samuel 11:14, Uriah refused to return home for even one night. Just one visit would have made Bathsheba's illicit pregnancy appear to be the natural result of their fidelity. But Uriah's stand for truth became an embarrassment to his cheating king. David took steps to eliminate Uriah. At last he married Uriah's widow and legitimized her pregnancy. The only reason David could consider this denigration was that he had depersonalized Uriah as a Gentile. Could David ever have arranged the tidy elimination if he had admitted Uriah's worth to God? So often our own personal agenda has caused us to forget how much God loves our antagonists. Uriah's Gentile status let David see him as expendable. How ugly must be those hidden prejudices that cause us to see our own socio-ethic status as more esteemed than that of others.

Conclusion

God made us to love people and use things. Why is it that we so often love things and use people? God longs to raise up those rare Christ-filled leaders who use their might to create right rather than claim that their might is right. How He longs for leaders who wield the politics of grace rather than those who become graceful politicians. God wants to raise up leaders who, united with Christ, become in all issues of decision-making indistinguishable from Christ.

Leadership: Coping with Difficult People

Power is always interpersonal.

Rollo May,
Power and Innocence

Baptista: Why then, thou canst not break her to the lute?
Hortensio: Why no, for she hath broke the lute to me.

William Shakespeare,
The Taming of the Shrew

I beseech Euodia,
and beseech Syntyche,
that they be of the same mind
in the Lord.

The Apostle Paul,
Epistle to the Philippians

Letter 8

Dear Leader:

When it comes to loving other people, you need to know that I fully agree with what Jean-Paul Sartre and Charlie Brown said. The former said, "Hell is other people," and the latter said, "I love humanity; it's people I can't stand."

I once had a pastor friend who answered my every query about the health of his church the very same way. Every time I asked him, "Bill, how's your church going?" he would always answer, "Just fine, now! We got rid of three more problem families this week." I followed his ministry very closely. In only three years he was completely out of problems . . . and members.

One pastor I read about had a similar approach to problems. He beamed that he had just had a "membership drive" in which he "drove" out fifteen families. They were all problem families, I'm sure.

Most people are problem people once in a while. In fact, nearly everybody is a problem to somebody, sometime, somewhere. You either solve these people problems or cope with them or ignore them or run them off. Pastor, I understand that in the ministry it gets hard to like everybody. Will Rogers did, I know, but then there's a general feeling that Will never got out much, and we know for sure he never pastored a church.

I'd like you to be like God. He loves everybody. Our problem people are just not problem people to Him. Pastor, if I turn out to be one of your problem people, I sure would like you to remember that. Clarence Darrow is famous for having said that he had never killed anybody, but that he had read many an obituary with pleasure. If I turn out to be one of your problem people and I happen to die before you do and you happen to preach my funeral, you don't have to cry. Just promise me you won't grin all the way through it.

—Your Follower

2 Samuel 21:1–14

All who lead must learn to cope with difficult people. The call to leadership demands that we learn that among those we lead exists a great many people who will be difficult, perhaps impossible, to lead. David, in 2 Samuel 21, has to settle a nettlesome problem that had gone on for years. The Gibeonites were difficult people with whom he had to cope. He knew they could not be ignored and their obstruction of his visions would not just evaporate. Beware of the sincerity myth that teaches that you will be able to avoid all criticism if only you are sincere.

The most disheartening time in the life of any rookie preacher is the first few weeks of service. This period of time can be debilitating and destructive to the soul. During college and seminary years, preachers find life consumed in the process of preparation. Then comes graduation! Suddenly the "preacher boy" is a full-fledged minister. The hard work of ministry begins. Maturity in any field is always hard-bought, but in the gospel ministry, it can be particularly difficult. Only in the ministry is it important that we lead unlovely people even as we try to see the character of Christ in their lives.

Many preachers, throughout seminary, continue to live with the adolescent delusion fostered by years of teen-age Christianity. During adolescence we all are shaped by the church and her message. Yet, during those years we are not deeply involved in the inner workings of the church. We look upon the church in our teens and tend to idealize its ministry. During these critical years of our formation, we are also especially sensitive of spirit. We are avid with desire to find out what our life careers should be. All in all, our adolescent delusions foster the impression that the church is really more perfect than it is. Our Christian calling is born during this impressionable time in our lives. Every church leader seems an icon of virtue. Every Christian appears to be a wonderful saint of God.

Observing these saints at an antiseptic distance, we never see their behavior at committee meetings. Nor do we imagine them at times of pastoral confrontation. Rather, we see them singing, praying and bearing testimony to love of Christ, just as we ourselves are doing in the youth department. In our youth, we do not always understand their addiction to the "old-fashioned Jesus." Their music is all unsingable hymns. Nor do we really understand their love of organs and choirs or their distaste for drum sets, amplifiers, and the other necessities. Still, from our uninvolved distance, they seem to be doing ministry entirely for their beloved, slow-paced Jesus while we are serving Him over in the fast lane.

In our teens we all go to youth camp. There on that special night a power team evangelist cuts a watermelon off the youth director's stomach with a samurai sword. Even as he cries, "Hai karate, Jesus!" we give our lives to the Lord, burning a kindling chip as a symbol of our living sacrifice. We sing the latest guitar and bongo chorus. Then, like The Hugenots (a word we will not learn until later years in our study of church history), we file to the flaming stake and throw our chip of wood in the fire. The smoke curls upward. Our call is fixed. We are martyrs, singing "Kum Ba Ya" while we wait for our time to die for Jesus.

We go back to church the next Sunday and announce our call publicly. Our father pats us on the back. Our mother cries and hugs us. The pastor really cries, for he understands what we cannot know about the life we are choosing. Thus, we enter the ministry. We study. Then all too soon seminary is over.

During the first few years of our ministry we learn why the pastor was crying. We begin to meet all those difficult people who intend to see that we arrive at our martyrdom right on time. Can these be the same souls who we once believed were so godly? Once we saw them only at their prayers. Now, we are seeing them at committee meetings.

Every great pastor must learn that problem people are customary and must be dealt with every day. So let us

139

begin this study by defining them. *Difficult people are those who stand between you and the realization of your objectives. They are a deterrent to the earliest possible achievement of your God-ordained dreams.*

It is helpful to remember that a heart crying to be loved lurks behind the obstinacy of many of these problem people. It is also good to remember that the best way to eliminate a critic is to make him or her your friend. Assuming these gentler techniques have been tried, however, problem people may have to be met on other bases.

Are they intentionally demonic? *Not at all.* They are just being people. While Jesus saves people and takes them all to heaven, it is a while before their more earthy attributes are purged.

The Chronically Arrogant

One type of person that is difficult to lead is the chronically arrogant. Chronically arrogant persons are often coping with removing inferiority. They are controlled by the delusion that their ideas are the only ones that matter. This type is not always brutal in relationships, but they are always strong-willed. Socrates believed that all of humanity could be divided into two types: the wise who know they are fools, and the fools who believe themselves to be wise. Chronically arrogant persons would fall into the latter category.

These chronically arrogant folk amount to what family manuals call strong-willed children. They are not altogether bad, but they have developed the chilling opinion that the church must revolve around them. If they are not included in board meetings, their opinions become self-fulfilling prophecies. As a pastor, I quickly learned that these demanding types were like plastic explosives. They stuck like gum on pews, leaving every church business conference a mine field of pending holocaust.

SIX DIFFICULT SOULS

CHRONICALLY ARROGANT
Burdens Leadership

CONGENITALLY BELLIGERENT
Declares War on Leadership

NON-NEGOTIATOR
Won't Inform Leadership

NIT-PICKER
Amends Greatness with Smallness

WHEEDLER
Needles Leadership Confidence

"YES-BUTTER"
Impedes Leadership

I could never really find any formula to stop them. Each new contender for the title of "Chronically Arrogant" was different from the last. But I quickly learned that they had to be stopped. I also learned that the pastor usually had to be the "stopper." They had to be stopped not so that they wouldn't destroy me. That was not generally their primary agenda. Their agenda was to get their way. In their oft-childlike way of seeing things, their way was best.

This is often where they come into conflict first with the leader, and later with the whole congregation. Pastors, too, are often blessed with ego, and indeed, some pastors themselves are chronically arrogant. After all, pastors are people too. They, like laypersons, may also fit any of the categories of this chapter. When a chronically arrogant pastor meets a chronically arrogant deacon, church difficulties can rise exponentially.

Since it is not their primary agenda to destroy the pastor, the pastor may be able to stop their takeover impulses with finesse. But however it is done, chronic-arrogants must be stopped. If they are not, the pastor may lose the leadership edge; indeed pastors who cannot control these types may in time lose their jobs.

But the worst thing that happens when the pastor cannot control these types is that the church is no longer free. The pastor is guilty of triumphalism when he wants to squelch them so that he can have his way instead.

The church never runs out of the chronically arrogant. Season by season, there is always a new batch hatching. Once out of the shell, they mature fast.

Often they are over-ambitious secondary officers in the big downtown corporations they cannot control. But they often do rise to become primary officers in the church that they often can control. When they become pushy in committee meetings, it gets hard to remember that they are not intentionally malicious. They are merely strong-willed. They just want to run things. Their maliciousness hides when they come to be in charge. So they must never be granted the license. Still, trying to honor their human side while checking their cannibalistic impulses is like taping a rose on a bulldozer.

Chronically arrogant people need to be taught that their ambition may really be their way of masking inferiority. But teaching them their psychological profile is risky. Cecil Osborne warns us: "It may be a source of confusion to some people to learn that ambition is a defense against the shame of inferiority, but, as it has been written, the truth will make you free, but first it may make you miserable. The bare truth can sometimes be shattering."[1] The best way to convince chronically arrogant persons of the value of humility is to wait. When life's hard circumstances come upon them, they are bruised into a learning status. I have found that this old parable of the lion helps me:

> A terrifying lion once met a cowardly monkey in the jungle. The lion pounced on the poor, shaking monkey and asked, as he breathed damnation in the monkey's face, "Who is the king of this jungle?"
>
> The monkey was terror-stricken and quickly acceded, "You are, O King!"
>
> The lion let him go.
>
> Next, the lion met an elephant. He roared out insults to the elephant, asking him the same question. The elephant was not so easily intimidated. With his trunk he picked up the lion and slammed him against a tree fifty feet away. The lion walked away and said very meekly, "Just because you don't know the answer is no reason to get rough."

Time often cures arrogance. People who play rough will, in time, meet someone even rougher. This encounter can tame their heavy-handedness and make them endurable.

As Christians, we are taught that "cheek turning" is the proper way to handle aggression. When dealing with a chronic-arrogant, I recommend trying Jesus' tactic. But blessing steamrollers may not be enough to protect the congregation. However we suppress their onslaught, it is important that we learn to deal with monsters without becoming monsters ourselves.

Congenitally Belligerent

Another difficult type of person with whom leaders must cope is the type I call congenitally belligerent. This category describes those people who have been upset since the womb. Congenitally belligerent people differ from the chronically arrogant who only wants to have his or her way. The congenitally belligerent are always aggressive and verbally abusive. Rough circumstances will not slow down the congenitally belligerent as they might the chronically arrogant. In fact, congenitally belligerent persons love fights and thrive on conflict.

Congenitally belligerents are always mad. Being eternally angry gives the congenitally belligerent a real edge in controlling church agendas. Anger makes others afraid. We learn early in childhood to be afraid of angry people.

Like the chronic-arrogant, however, congenital-belligerents will quickly take over a committee or a congregation. Their first line of offense may be hot words that strip the more gentle of courage. Leaders tend to fear these congenitally belligerents. But true leaders must pick up their courage. Angry people are, after all, just people. To get them out of their fearsome mode, fearsome challenges must be given.

In some ways, a congenitally belligerent woman is more difficult to handle than a man because her husband will often stand up and fight for her. Further, it is very hard for most men to openly confront a woman. For most feminists there is a tendency to see all chivalry that fosters kindness as male supremacy and sexist oppression. Every male minister has, in his collection of congregation war stories, a tale of such a woman. My nemesis for a couple of years was "Joni." In all my years of knowing her, I never saw her smile even during the singing of "joy" choruses or during praise time. She was always mad. She sang mad hymns and prayed mad prayers. The only time I ever heard her give her testimony it was a mad testimony. When I was in my car I would occasionally see her driving to the supermarket. Even through the windshield of her car she looked sour. She even drove mad. It was difficult to stop her in church, but gradually the lioness was tamed. She eventually left our church in anger and joined another in anger. And while I felt sorry for that new gathering of saints she had found to persecute, it was good to see a smiling face in her pew. Gone, gloriously gone was her face, as stony and cold as Mt. Rushmore in winter.

It is unlikely that your most conscientious efforts will bring even a momentary sweetness of spirit to such people. David Seamands relates how someone very close to one such person remarked: "Joyce, you certainly are an even-tempered person—you're always mad."[2] Seamands also tells about a congenitally belligerent person who was described as having *colitis.* Overhearing the remark about *colitis,* a little boy asked, "Who's she been colliding with now?"

Congenitally belligerent people are always colliding with someone. In every organization, they are always colliding with the leader. Effective leaders must take the collisions head-on, assuring these difficult individuals that they can gain nothing through bullying and belligerence. You must handle their belligerence firmly. You must convey that you understand that they are persons for whom Christ died, but that you too are a person.

Norm Evans tells about a football lineman who had a problem with an opposing lineman. He took the problem to his coach saying, "He keeps pulling my helmet over my eyes. What should I do?"

The coach wisely answered, "Don't let him do it!"[3]

Congenitally belligerent people must be stopped! Another motivator refers to congenitally belligerent people as Sherman tanks. They must never be allowed to roll over the organization, crushing others beneath their titanic self-importance.

The Non-Negotiator

I call this third type of difficult person the non-negotiator. These persons uniquely confront our leadership. Non-negotiators usually remain quiet in an attempt to keep away from all organizational transactions, but their silence is not demurring; their silence is an act of aggression. It is intended to diminish the opportunity for others to share. David Augsburger calls this negative communication and says that "silence, avoidance, evasion, and absence may show disagreement or even anger without confrontation. 'I did not answer' may mean 'I objected.' Silence, which may have many meanings from social reserve to sulking, can communicate what the person intends without the threat of invasion, and its negative implications can be denied if it is challenged."[4] By refusing all negotiation, they are inaccessible and can block all progress with their silence. Non-negotiators must be confronted in as frank a way as possible and be made to disseminate what they know would advance the project.

Just as silence can be used by non-negotiators, so can whining. Whining is a ploy used consistently by many problem people to avoid negotiation. Whiners use whining to bend commiseration in their direction. Thus whining non-negotiators are often powerful persons. These do not whine to get their grievance answered. They whine because it gives them an edge in controlling business relationships. As a leader you usually can never make these people happy by acceding to their demands. Their real demand has nothing to do with your conciliation. They are not after control, but recognition. They do not want to run things, they just want the spotlight. They cause no real harm, except they often distract the major agenda of the church demanding that it console them.

Margaret Beeson was like that in my ministry. It was always dangerous to ask about her health. One really did not have time for the answer. She was not only too diseased to be brief, she was too diseased to be interesting. She had a way of describing her various maladies that deadened the eardrums with an awful, slow-paced whine.

She always needed to go somewhere for therapy but she had no car of her own. She also needed medicine from time to time. Her whining always laid a healthy dose of guilt on all who denied her help. After all, what kind of minister of Christ would deny a suffering woman a short drive to the pharmacist (the only one she really trusted was twenty-five miles across town)? It would be ungodly to refuse to buy her the drugs that she needed. How often, as I drove her home from the pharmacist, I wondered if taking her drugs might help me endure her whining mystique.

But it was mostly what she did in prayer session and business meetings that killed the agenda of the church. Margaret was a part of our congregation before we became large. Non-negotiators in small congregations can whine their way into positions of real power. Just walking into our prayer meeting smelling like medicine, she reminded all of us to pray for her. At business meetings, she, like all non-negotiators, hardly said a thing, but the private work she did on the phones prior to the meetings could quietly set the agenda for the whole church. She was hard to criticize, being a "frail" woman who so often needed the deacon council at her sickbed.

The difficulty in dealing with this type of person is that they really seem to be in pain. Their aim is to make you feel especially heartless if you confront them. But make no mistake about it, manipulating your feelings is their intentional ploy. Even though they appear Christlike and needy, they must not be allowed to delay the objectives of the leadership team.

The Nitpicker

One of the difficult types most irritating to me is one I call the nitpicker. Nitpickers have a way of majoring on minor issues that can distract the congregation from its mission. A friend of mine who once pastored a rural Oklahoma congregation described the nitpickers in a most interesting way. He said that when his daughter was very little, the hot Oklahoma August was sweltering to the baby. Her little body would be tortured with a heat rash that, coupled with the flies, mosquitoes, and unrelieved temperatures, would make life nearly unbearable for the child.

Sometimes, so that she would have some relief from the heat, they would take her shirt off of her, leaving her dressed only in her diaper. Then they would put her in her highchair and give her an ice cube to play with. Her highchair had a white steel tray. Since the metal tray was also hot, the ice cube would melt rather rapidly even as she tried to pick it up. Undaunted, the child tried again and again to pick it up. As her chubby little fingers tried to grasp the ever diminishing cube, it squirted out of her fingers. Pinching the ice around the tray, she was never quite able to get hold of it. She would pursue it until it was only a spiraling trail of water on the tray. She had "nitpicked" away all the substance. How often I have seen church persons making mountains out of molehills, until the church had arrived at a way of life that was only a maintenance project. Nitpickers pursue no *major* dreams. Nit-picking ignores big ideas until the church's vision is eroded. They eat away the noble center of every dream. The nitpicker must be constantly challenged to focus on things that really matter.

The Wheedler

Someone has suggested that the word *wheedler* is like the word *cockapoo*, a hybrid word combining whiner and needler. The wheedler whines and groans to have his or her way. This difficult type is similar to the non-negotiator but is more communicative. Wheedlers negotiate, but they always use a grieving tone the moment you force them from their complaint. Their whining can be so unpleasant that others will let them have their way rather than risk the unpleasantness of listening to them lose.

Wheedlers, like all non-negotiators, don't do much. Their sole calling seems to be sure that the attention of the church keeps focused on them. Then, if by no other means, they step up the whining and wheedling until they forbid the attention to go anywhere else. I remember Diana who came to the membership of our church complaining that the last church to which she belonged had never ministered to her in an adequate way. She loved our church because we were more "filled with the Spirit of Christ" than her last church. It is generally true that people who arrive at a new church complaining about their old church will someday leave taking that same complaint to yet another church. This was indeed the case of Diana.

She attracted all of our attention by complaining of her last church, and she was immediately gratified that our church had noticed her great need for ministry. Ministry, in her case, included some financial needs (we often paid her rent) and physical needs (we often bought her medicine for her poor health). She also had many spiritual needs: she was from a dysfunctional family, and her children had disowned her. At first we thought her children were cruel, but later we wondered. In time, the church wearied with her incessant implorings. As they began to see her whining, needling nature, they cut back on help. She then began to be more and more dissatisfied with the church, and ultimately went to another church that was "more filled with the Spirit of Christ" than ours.

Wheedlers are aware of the psychological power of their demeanor. Seeing others retreat often hastens their negative aggression. Do not be naive! Wheedlers are not innocent about their ability to invoke guilt in other Christians. Herb Bisno counsels us that "the stimulation of guilt in another person, as a mode of influence, is not an uncommon form of 'emotional blackmail.' It is likely to occur in close primary relationships, or where there is a strong collective bond among members of a group or organization."[5] As a leader, you can challenge a wheedler by asking, "Can you state your feelings about this more positively?" or "Aren't you happy today?" or "Must you be so melodramatic?" or "Let's have the facts only. We'll decide if we want to feel as negatively about this as you do."

The "Yes-Butter"

The yes-butter is a difficult person who greets every great idea by saying, "Yes, but it won't work for this reason." This type is easy to spot because the word *but* always immediately follows the word *yes*. Also called nay-sayers, they can point out aspects of an issue or project that are likely to go wrong, so it is often good to listen to them. Unfortunately, their heavy negativity is often a blockade for everything right. Therefore it is best to use them for private advice or place them in a less conspicuous role where their negativity will have little influence on great decisions. "When negativism reigns, any disagreement becomes bad," says John Vale. "He may tend to spend too much time analyzing what is wrong and spending little or no time analyzing what is right."[6] This type of person must be asked to state feelings without prejudicing others about the outcome.

Conclusion

There are four logical questions that need to be answered to tell how we are coping with these various types of people.

First we need to ask, "Why has God sent these persons into my life?" Often it is the most demanding and the least recompensing people who waken our need to grow in Christ. David's reckoning with the Gibeonites teaches us that there is much to be learned by such reckoning (see 2 Sam. 21:1ff).

The second question that needs to be asked is, "Which old enemies should be sought out for reconciliation?" In one lifetime there is not usually time to work to develop or repair all of the broken relationships that we encounter. David, in 2 Samuel 21:2, makes it clear that he picked the Gibeonites to try to help at least one group of his ancient enemies overcome the vitriol of their grudge for him.

FOUR KEY QUESTIONS IN ANALYZING OUR COPING EFFICIENCY

Why has God sent this particular problem person into my life?

Which of my problem people can be reconciled to the corporate dream?

How far can I go to satisfy the grudges of antagonists?

When is my time better spent on finding new support rather then trying to "sweeten up" old belligerence?

The second question is always the immediate preface to a third: "How far should we go to satisfy the grudges of an old enemy?" David knew that the restored people would infiltrate his kingdom and spread the greatest amount of discord that they could. This must have led David to reason that it is not possible to make everyone happy in life. He then had to decide who he should choose and how hard he should work at it.

The fourth question is one of necessity: "When problem people become too severe, are they worthy of the effort? When is our time better spent recruiting new support than trying to sweeten up old antagonists?" These are key questions. There is a great deal of time required in changing the types described above. I always found that once a church member states his or her intention to leave, it is all but impossible to claim them. No matter what the church and the pastor tried to do, they would at last "walk." Nonetheless, this final attempt must be made and all that can be kept and prayed for should be.

Perhaps there is a final issue that must be addressed. It is always possible that we who do the leading might actually be considered a difficult person for others in the congregation. It behooves each of us who lead to be sure that our walk with Christ is sufficient to keep us from being a stumbling block for someone else. The successful Christian leader must not only handle all of these difficult types, he or she must realize that even the most difficult people are loved by God. Everyone has a right to dignity. So the key issue in coping with difficult people is to handle them without belittling them before others. Love is a key ingredient of leadership. Even in the direst circumstances, any sort of rebuke should be as private as possible. Leaders must honestly determine if a person causing trouble is really difficult. They may only be trying to express a difficulty with some issue at hand. Difficult people and people with difficulties are two different things. Great leaders study and understand both.

Leaders have to build their worlds with the materials at hand. David's kingdom was surrounded by evil circumstances inherited from a previous regime. Throughout David's reign, these preexisting conditions continually surfaced, always causing him difficulty. As a leader, David had to deal not only with future issues, but with the ghosts of troubles that had plagued the kingdom long before he even began to lead it. So will it ever be in the church.

At a recent church business conference where I am serving as the interim pastor, the church voted 1,235 to 17 in favor of calling a certain new pastor. The retiring pastor, who left after eighteen years of glorious ministry, said, "I'll bet it was the same seventeen who voted against me when I came." We laughed at his summation of these seventeen negative votes, but we did not laugh long.

Leadership:
The Art of Delegation
and Team Spirit

In the best-selling book,
In Search of Excellence,
the authors point out that
the best run companies in America
invariably have employees
who share the pride of the corporate name.

David L. McKenna,
Renewing Our Ministry

Speak for yourself, John.

Henry Wadsworth Longfellow,
"The Courtship of Miles Standish"

Now this is the law of the jungle,
It's as old and as true as the sky,
And the wolf that shall keep it may prosper
And the wolf that shall break it must die.
As the creeper that girdles the tree trunk,
The truth runneth forward and back,
For the strength of the pack is the wolf,
And the strength of the wolf is the pack.

Rudyard Kipling,
"The Law of the Jungle"

Letter 9

Dear Leader:

When I was a little boy, I wanted to play baseball in the city youth league. I was sure proud when I got my uniform and cap, two weeks before our first practice session. I wore it around everywhere—to school, to church, on shopping trips with my mother. But after that first practice, I felt very bad. My coach had noticed that, while I looked good in my uniform, I could not catch the ball. I was not a good batter, and I was a poor thrower. This trio of faults the team recognized as a triple threat.

Still the coach thought he saw some potential in me. He gave me special attention. He spent many extra hours with me each week. After a whole summer of his special attention, I still could not throw the ball or catch the ball, and I remained a poor batter. When the other kids yelled at the coach for putting me in the game, he'd set me down squarely in center field, knowing full well that every fly ball that came near me I would drop. When I struck out, he would pat me on the head and say, "Nice clear swings!" He patted me on the head just like he patted Billy Simmons, who hit at least one home run per game.

But best of all, when the coach treated us to ice-cream cones after our winning games, I always got a double dip just like everyone else. It's hard to feel like a loser when you're licking ice-cream cones with the champions. I was a part of a winning team, and the coach let everyone know it too.

Well Pastor, you've probably noticed by now that I can't sing very well. I also won't make a very good Sunday School teacher. I've never been very good at public speaking. Actually, I've always been shy in front of a group. I don't have a very high paying job, so my tithe is not going to be much help. But before I join your church, I gotta know, "Do I still get an ice-cream cone after the game?"

—Your Follower

2 Samuel 23:8–17

Good leaders never give their leadership away. However, they do share both the rewards and responsibilities of leading. One of the outstanding Bible passages on this concept is in Exodus 18:21–22 where Jethro (Moses' father-in-law) noticed Moses' extreme fatigue and suggested that Moses not try to do all of the counseling in the camp of Israel by himself. Jethro's solution was to suggest that Moses delegate some of his counseling load to others.

Often a company or a church consists of a few hassled, harried leaders and a great many take-it-easy followers. Generally, such followers have not been challenged to participate in bearing the workload of those who lead, and no great leader can live long in this condition. Followers must be made to believe they are a part of a team. They must be made to participate with the leader in the work the team has to do. Such participation will level out both the busyness at the top and the lackadaisical attitude at the bottom. Less than one of four working people now say they are working at full potential. Half of the current workforce say that they do not put any more effort into a job than they absolutely must do to keep the job. Three-fourths of the American workforce say they could be more effective, and almost 60 percent agree that they do not work as hard as they used to work.[1]

Leadership vs. Management

"Most organizations are underled and overmanaged," says Warren Bennis.[2] This must certainly be true of churches as well. Bennis also gives us the simplest and best of all definitions of leadership and management. "Leaders are people who do the right thing but managers are those who do things right."[3]

Leadership and management are two very different commodities. Leadership has to do with direction and management with organizing and mobilizing an organization to go in that direction.

DISTINGUISHING
LEADERSHIP AND MANAGEMENT

LEADERSHIP SAYS	MANAGEMENT SAYS
Where we're going	How we get there
Look	Act
There is your destiny	Here is your roadmap
Here's an architect's rendering of Oz	Follow the yellow brick road

Stephen Covey says that management organizes a jungle task force to use machetes to hack their way through the thick forest of corporate agenda. Management will designate separate parts of the jungle crew to be "machete sharpeners." Managers appoint other jungle committees to count the hours of machete use. Still others are sent to measure how much forest gets cut in terms of the total hours spent chopping. Further control groups determine the quality of jungle cutting that really gets done. But leadership never preoccupies itself with machetes. Leadership climbs a tall tree and looks around and shouts down to machete management such things as "Wrong jungle!"

Leaders must keep in touch with management and in a small, single staff church, obviously the pastor must lead—that is, set the direction for the church, and also must manage—that is, organize the church to move in the right direction. But the management process can be organized in six steps. Joe Batten suggests that these six steps to better management should be taken in this order.

Research should precede planning. Planning should precede organizing. After all are organized, we must learn to direct, coordinate, and control.[4]

The process of management must always end with a quantitative and qualitative measurement of what has been achieved. But the wideness of achievement will always come in direct proportion to the leader's aptitude at delegation.

Good Leadership Delegation

You can never achieve great leadership without effective delegation. By delegation, you will increase the job commitment of others by spreading your task effectively over a broader base. As others feel more responsible for the work, they begin to care about the outcome. But in order to build a true team spirit, you must delegate accountability and glory as well as responsibility. Because of our human selfishness, it is clear that accountability and glory are far harder to delegate than responsibility. Still, you can never arrive at the top plateau of leadership by insisting that others do all the work while you take all the glory. A leader must be a team player.

Real leaders make followers accountable for the tasks they delegate. When a task is finished, any fault that has accrued will belong to those who were in charge of the assignment. It is also wise to remember that your followers' ability to accept the pain of their failure or the glory of their success is directly related to the role model you supply. If you bear your responsibility in an accountable way, those to whom you have delegated a task will imitate your stewardship.

By delegation I am not suggesting that a leader shrug off his or her responsibilities. To do such would be to commit what Joe Batten considers an abdication of leadership. He clearly distinguishes between delegation and abdication. "*Delegation* means to assign, trust, instruct. If needed, provide for orderly and mutually agreed upon feedback with the full realization that you are still accountable for seeing that team members understand and fulfill their responsibility, authority, and accountability. *Abdication* means to relinquish all control and follow through, and hope the assignment gets done."[5]

David's ability to delegate is seen in 2 Samuel 23:8–17. Those mentioned there were worthy of honor in David's monarchy. David both shared the task and, when the work was done, the glory. David's commendation of his "mighty men of valor" suggests that he was not the only person allowed to wear such titles in Israel. David's generous spirit is the hallmark of every true leader. He could share the load and yet remain a team player.

Studying the life of David in chronological sequence, it is hard to know where to put 2 Samuel 23. It makes some sense to place its events near the end of King David's long reign. In that context, the passage portrays the old king reflecting over his youth and recalling the various team members who in days gone by had helped him subdue the land. However, these same events are also recorded in 1 Chronicles 11:11–47, where they are placed after the capturing of the citadel (Jerusalem). I have decided to locate this important event chronologically after 2 Samuel 5, which deals with the young king as he occupies his new capital for the first time.

Regardless of where we place the events of this passage chronologically, its message remains one of leadership and team spirit. Only the deeds of three of the thirty knights are spelled out. But the passage indicates that all were equally important. As David reflected on their deeds, he named each man, and we learn the importance of team loyalty.

David began the designation of his thirty knights with three who seemed to be very special to him. Those special people whose team playing help frame our careers comprise the networks we talked about in chapter 3. Networking and delegating go hand in hand. Those who cannot or will not delegate wind up aloof and out of touch with their community. Their entire lives and careers are mired in ego.

But why would any leader refuse to learn the art of delegation? Because those who will not delegate are so insecure they cannot admit the necessity of the team. Like a stage-struck quarterback, they must carry every ball, on every play. They must be the one who scores at every goal line. Why? Because they can't stand for anyone else to have any glory in the game.

There may be one other reason for Lone Ranger leadership. Some leaders who cannot delegate can share the glory. However, they do not do so, because they cannot figure out how to share the glory with others and still make their own way in the corporate structure. They care so much for their own advancement that they appear to lack administrative know-how. So some cannot delegate because of insecurity. Some will not delegate because of ambition.

But both end up, at last, struggling with self. Are the persons who are too insecure to delegate and too ambitious to delegate both struggling with ego? Yes. Neither type may be inherently selfish. Still, either type becomes a one-man band depriving their organization of team spirit and corporate celebration. Nor does either type learn this truth: When delegation is applied, every organization becomes stronger. Let's consider the first three of David's mighty men.

Adino the Eznite

Adino the Eznite is definitely the quarterback of David's team. He did a great job (see 2 Sam. 23:8). In fact, he was the star.

Every team has its favorite corporate star. The star wears the right clothes and closes the right deals. Without these show-off all-stars, high-agenda leaders feel isolated. These movers and shakers appeal to the CEOs who groom them for boardroom portraits. In the world of religion, these pastors are often the stars of the church-growth firmament. They coin the vocabulary and set the standards for emulation. They are so successful, they glitter. They challenge, intimidate, and model all things bright and beautiful. One gets the feeling that Joab may have been such a superstar in David's cabinet. Even Uriah, before his murder, may have been such a supporter and confidante to the king. In this particular listing of David's Fortune 500, it is Adino the Eznite who kills many Philistines. What's left to say except, "Bully for Adino!"

Eleazar, the Son of Dodai

Giving Adino the Eznite his due, consider the commitment of Eleazar, the son of Dodai (see 2 Sam. 23:9–10). He fought for David until his hand "clave to the sword." His support and commitment to his king are without question. With outstanding quarterbacks like Eleazar, one wonders whether all that Adino meant to the organization came from his commitment or his native talent and education. But Eleazar leaves little doubt that his chief virtue is commitment.

Delegation finds rich rootage in loyalty. Elmer Gantry, in the novel by Sinclair Lewis, is defended and protected by T. J. Rigg. The novel reaches a lofty sentiment in the utter pledge of this committed layman to his pastor. The Rev. Mr. Gantry was not all that pure in spirit. Still, one cannot read the novel without being convinced that Gantry is a leader. His success was due in a large part to the loyalty of a man who will not let him lead alone. When I think of biblical loyalty, I am reminded of Ephesians 6:5–8:

> Slaves, obey your earthly masters with respect and fear, and with sincerity of heart, just as you would obey Christ. Obey them not only to win their favor when their eye is on you, but like slaves of Christ, doing the will of God from your heart. Serve wholeheartedly, as if you were serving the Lord, not men, because you know that the Lord will reward everyone for whatever good he does, whether he is slave or free. (NIV)

The most loyal people are those who serve Christ for eternal reward. They do not serve Him because they want to be considered among the spiritually elite.

This may be a far reach to compare Eleazar with T. J. Rigg. It is not much of a reach to compare Eleazar with Bob H., the most commendable man of character I have ever known. Bob is the arch example of commitment, first of all to God and second to me, his pastor.

Bob was a master of all things architectural. He was so instrumental in the unfolding design of our church building that I found myself relying totally on his expertise. My admiration always expressed itself to our congregation. On the other hand, Bob saw me as a Bible scholar and preacher. His influence in the city allowed him to bring some of the most notable civic leaders to our church. He brought them to hear me preach. Gradually we became a team. We felt God had brought us together. Together we built a large congregation and a beautiful building. Because of our mutual commitment to each other, our joint leadership led us through a period of unparalleled accomplishments. I will always be grateful for what he taught me about loyalty and commitment. Near the end of my twenty-five-year ministry, he was killed in a traffic accident. At the time of his death, I had no idea that I would be leaving the pastoral ministry within two years, and I grieved his passing. I had lost a soul mate! I continued to miss the Eleazar-like quality of his commitment.

Shammah, the Son of Agee

Of these three knights, Shammah, mentioned in 2 Samuel 23:11–12, is the most curious. He is celebrated for defending a lentil field. He does an admirable job of dispatching the enemy in a none-too-admirable place. Among David's mighty men, Shammah is a minor hero. These minor heroes fill our churches. Yet in every sense, the Shammahs of church leadership are worthy of praise. They give diligent attention to those little things out of which life in the church is composed. Minor players always hold the major number of roles in every organization. They well deserve to be called heroes, even if their roles seem minor.

Great followers are those who are faithful in dispatching their lowly responsibilities. In every war there are minor battles, battles in bean fields. Shammah is celebrated by the king for the faithful execution of his assignment. Doing little jobs with megasized commitment is the glory of those saints we tend to overlook.

I have long believed that my mother was one of these saints. I will always remember her funeral. She had one of the largest I have ever seen. Several times, as I heard the pastor read her eulogy, I asked myself why. For her entire life she had done nothing more than be faithful to a small assignment. She was a nursery worker throughout all her years of association with the church. She never once in all those years held a major church office. She never once gave even a church committee report. She never made a motion or offered a second in any business meeting. I suppose that in that entire score of years she kept the nursery she never missed her appointed time of service.

Why would so many attend a nursery worker's funeral? I continued to ponder the question for years. In time I came to serve my own church as a pastor. It, in time, became a large church. It was desperately hard to find those who would be faithful to their service in the nursery. My mother had given her life in a real "towel-and-basin" way. I at last discovered what Shammah must have taught all of Israel from a bean field. Uncommon faithfulness to common jobs is an uncommon glory.

The Team's Dependability

Every leader leads by team building. Whether the team we build is really dependable will be based largely on our communication skills. Leaders must ask themselves, "How do I come across in communicating the direction and vision for my church or organization?" Bert Decker says there are nine factors in effectively communicating to the corporate team (on the following page). Four of these are eye factors, four are energy factors, and the final factor is probably most critical of all. How do we become our natural selves in communicating with the team? We do it in two ways. We look them in the eye and speak to them with gusto. We will develop these communication skills more fully as we grow older. As these skills mature, we will become ever more seasoned in our leadership style. Concerning the importance of teamwork, Jim Lundry writes: "Real teamwork can be so gratifying that it may be considered reward enough. Nevertheless, the individual who habitually communicates, cooperates, and collaborates with others will be recognized by his or her associates as an invaluable asset."[6]

DECKER'S EYE AND ENERGY FACTORS OF COMMUNICATION

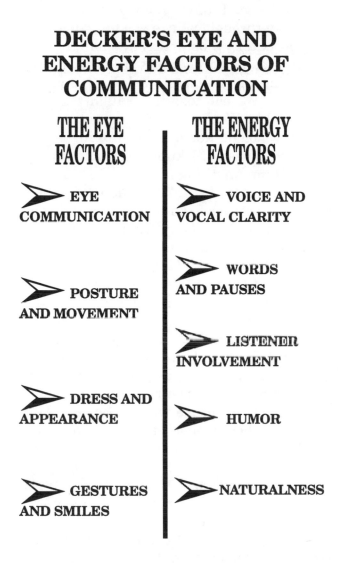

THE EYE FACTORS

➤ EYE COMMUNICATION

➤ POSTURE AND MOVEMENT

➤ DRESS AND APPEARANCE

➤ GESTURES AND SMILES

THE ENERGY FACTORS

➤ VOICE AND VOCAL CLARITY

➤ WORDS AND PAUSES

➤ LISTENER INVOLVEMENT

➤ HUMOR

➤ NATURALNESS

Some of our brash acts of camaraderie occur when we are young. It is during our youthful years that we form many of those segments of our networks that survive to serve us all of our lives. Some of those old fraternity brothers, who pledge to be "friends till death" on graduation day, actually remain so. I have such a friend. Together we worked our way through college washing dishes in the college cafeteria. Later we both served small, northern Oklahoma churches as pastors. Across these past forty years, I have called him many times to ask for his counsel. He is now my pastor. We eat together, laugh together, talk to each other weekly. We rarely criticize each other. Friendship, as it grows older, has less need to inspect or critique each other's weaknesses. I know he would do almost anything I ask of him. Anything he asks of me, I too would do. Is such a statement too brash? I think not . . . ever! No good friend ever asks another to do something that is beyond his or her means to perform. Only when circumstances are so suffocating that they kill does a truly good friend impose upon our lives by calling, "Help me!" Still, a good friend would rather hurt with you than ever see you suffer alone.

As recently as two years ago I was considering a job change. Resigning my twenty-six-year pastorate left me with an advanced case of the heebie-jeebies. I was torn up inside. It was difficult to leave a congregation whose lives had been interwoven into my own for so long. At least twice a week I called my old college friend. He was four decades wiser than he was when we were in college. He was also chairman of the board of a private university that had made overtures toward hiring me as their dean. I had decided not to take the job at his university, instead preferring a simple teaching job at the seminary. I wondered if I had appeared ungrateful in refusing the generous job he offered. If so, it never showed. He warmly dismissed my rejection of his job offer and counseled me to take the job he personally preferred that I not take. My own career agony was never met with harshness, only counsel. What I like best about this friend is that he understands my insecurities, a malady from which he rarely suffers. He loves me in spite of my hang-ups. He is a valuable part of my life team.

I want to distinguish the life team from a mere *network*. A network can be a symbiotic friendship. It will serve us as we serve it. A life team member, however, is more unconditional in its love of us. It does not merely exist to feed us as it gets fed. There is no measurement of the size of the last favor extended. It lies waiting and ready to help, no matter how long it has been since the last time we asked it for help. Unlike a network member, a life team player never asks, "What have you done for me lately?" There is no "lately," no requirement, no sense of necessary recompense. There are no emotionally charged receipts. Life together is the only payback.

I have a fellow artist who is a life team member. We worked together early in our careers in many art shows. We galleried together. Most lately in our lives we have written children's books together. His attendance to me is phenomenal. He calls, we talk; even across these past twenty years, we cannot stop sharing the pain in our process nor the heat in our glorious hot ideas. We like Shakespeare together, theater of all sorts, books, and quiet lunches. We are both "off the wall," as others define us, but merely "where the action is," as we define ourselves. Through such friends as he, I am able to survive and keep my best ideas moving through to some sort of completion.

Second Samuel 23:15–17 seems to refer to a time in David's life when he was quite young. He was probably in flight from Saul. This Scripture signet must be quite out of sequence as it appears here, at the end of David's life. Bethelehem, his home town, is under Philistine occupation. Further, the nature of this tale is boyish, brash, and braggart. It is the kind of thing young warriors would think up laughing like Falstaff in an alehouse.

David has to have a drink from the well in Bethlehem. Bethlehem is under foreign garrison. Nonetheless, the prank is taken seriously. At much risk to themselves, his friends go to Bethlehem to get David a drink. No harm comes to his soldiers, but when David understands the risk he has put them under, he is ashamed. He pours out the water that could have cost them their lives. He understands that his practical joke could have cost him his life team friendships.

David's penance at his folly is obvious. So it is with all great leaders who take lightly the welfare of those who make their leadership effective. The passage most celebrates the dependability of great life team players. Between the years of their bringing their king this dangerous flask of water and the time of his mentioning it must be forty years. But then, a good team is like that.

Our mates should be the closest of our life team members. They will either support us, making possible a kind of glorious achievement, or they will bar us from success altogether. I am a friend of Madeleine L'Engle. Anyone who knows her knows how much credit she gave to her husband Hugh Franklin. Hugh was an actor all his life and knew some achievement in the arts on his own. But in many ways, he was never destined to achieve her status. Yet he never seemed to abandon her in moments of discouragement. During those early years when she so much needed someone to believe in her, he was there for her. Before she won the Newberry Award, her manuscript, *A Wrinkle in Time*, had been rejected forty times. It was Hugh's life team support that made her a survivor in those days. She could never quit trying because of his unfailing faith in her. Following Hugh's death, her wonderful book, *Two-Part Invention*, made it clear just how well his support had served.

Her testimony of Hugh is my testimony of Barbara. Whatever quality of life I seem to produce, I know that my wife of thirty-five years is likely the reason. I know that her unflagging, deliciously blind confidence leads her to believe that my last pages are the best I have ever written. I bait her to supply me with confidence. When she says these words are great, I always ask, "Do you really think so!" She always does.

Like Hugh Franklin to Madeleine L'Engle, Barbara in those critical early years of my writing stood by me, encouraging me to go on. I did, but often with flagging hope. One day, in that morose period of my life, I received one more crushing rejection. My first (as yet unpublished) manuscript came back to me for the fifth time. I could see Barbara was clearly angry at "those idiots at the publishing house." Why were they so inexcusably blind? Why couldn't they see my obvious genius? Like Cassandra on the walls of Troy, she held the newly rejected manuscript in her hand. Brandishing it, sword-like, she said, "These people are going to be so sorry some day. Some day they will beg to print anything by you. Don't you give them a thing. Not a thing, do you hear me? Make them pay for their ignorance!"

I was only thirty at the time, and she was barely twenty-five. But our life team commitments were already in force.

Leadership needs a life team friend. Lee Iaccoca also cites his wife as that unceasing support that has made his vast achievements possible. The life team support of our spouses knows one other glory: intimacy. I use the word quite independent of its sexual mooring. Intimacy is that closeness that bonds our lives with caresses and physical nearness. We touch. The touch alone tells us that we are one in life. We share ideas, work acrostics, read the same book, and share the same theater. We know in the unfolding years of simple mornings that our togetherness goes beyond the threshold of mere networking. It has a splendor far above the remoteness of being just a life team. It is unspeakable oneness and this intimate bonding is glory! It declares our utter significance to one other person and thus to ourselves.

This intimacy slices the future wide open, as casually as it slices a grapefruit. It pours out its life in sacrifice as it comfortably pours the coffee. It makes a cup of tea and says, "If I can help it, all of life for you will be just this . . . a cup of tea." Max DePree is more than correct when he states that "intimacy rises from translating personal and corporate values into daily work practices, from searching for knowledge and wisdom and justice. Above all, intimacy rises from, and gives rise to, strong relationships."[7]

The real fountain of our success lies at the merger of two streams: the support of our life team—often same-gender friends—and those special mates God has given us. Where the counsel of trusted friend and a committed mate meet, we are made wealthy in both the quality and endurance of our leadership.

Good Leadership: Adjustment in Management Style

No matter how well we delegate or pick good team players, every leader is at the mercy of his or her own flexibility. If you cannot adjust as your organization grows, you will soon be obsolete. My experience in helping a church grow from 10 to 3,000 members has taught me that I was both the greatest motivator and yet the single greatest enemy to our continued forward progress. At every plateau of membership size, I knew I had to adjust to the growing size of the church administration task. At a larger size, I had to vary my style of administration. Leadership adjustment is always imperative as organizations grow.

Change is a big word! Change is readily seen as a great asset by those who honor the tolerance and understanding of your leadership. It will only be seen as fickleness if you have been intolerant toward others. David McKenna wrote in *The Psychology of Jesus,* "People grow and change by stops, starts, jumps, and fallbacks along a trend line. Ross Mooney, a psychologist friend, once compared human development to the exercise of walking. A body is in balance when standing still. In order to walk, however, imbalance must be risked as one foot moves forward. In that state of disequilibrium, the body has a natural drive for stability; so the trailing foot is signaled forward and balance is regained."[8] Still, most leaders greet change reluctantly.

I think leaders are afraid of what I call the four demons of doubt.

> Demon #1: Ignorance. I don't know how to handle this situation. If only I'd gotten an MBA.
>
> Demon #2: Heredity. I can't change because this is how God made me. If God had made me more flexible instead of so stubborn, I would be able to adjust.
>
> Demon #3: Age. I'm getting too old to really handle these continual adjustments.
>
> Demon #4: Inferiority. I can't do this. Who am I to consider this?
>
> And these demons can be driven out by a single rebuke, "Oh fiddlesticks! Here goes!"

Every adjustment in leadership style means the leader can see that the direction of his or her leadership is off course. Rather than continuing to lead in the wrong direction, the leader is making a correction mid-course.

In management style, most leaders realize that organizational growth wars against the closeness of relationships. Changes enlarge structures and leave distances between friends. Church growth says to all concerned, "The way we have felt about each other and reacted to each other may have to change for the benefit of the common task we serve."

Most denominational churches are not growing. In fact, seventy-nine percent of Southern Baptist churches are either static or in decline. What great deterrent keeps churches from growing? I believe some of this lack of growth can be attributed to a failure on the part of individual pastors or leaders to adjust their management styles.

One church growth expert says most churches will not grow beyond a two-person staff because most pastors are too insecure. These insecure leaders cannot share the glory of congregational veneration with more than one other person. Such pastors' psychological need for esteem leaves them unable to release enough of their specific control to enable their congregations to grow.

David of Bethlehem must have gone through the same kinds of needful changes as he grew from a renegade, guerrilla fighter to a real monarch. As we examine his management style, let's pay particular attention to David's ways of relating to his followers as Jerusalem grows from a small Jebusite city to a capital of empire.

Every change in the organization means that a leader must adjust and manage in a different way than before the change occurred. In 2 Samuel 21:15–22, it becomes clear that Israel had grown to the place where David had to change his methodology. He could no longer govern exactly as he did when he was a mountain chieftain fleeing from Saul. David demonstrated three principles of management style that every leader must consider if his leadership is to grow and expand.

Overcoming Fatigue in a Growing Organization

A lot of attention is given to burnout these days. Burnout results from psychological overload. It is often a hostile, fatigued withdrawal from responsibility. In 2 Samuel 21, David is much older than he is in 1 Samuel 17 when he goes up against Goliath. Goliath was met in the strength and passion of his youth, and he handled that responsibility very well. But now, in 2 Samuel 21, there are new giants to be fought and David is older. He gets tired so much easier than he once did. The King James Version of the Bible says that David "waxed faint" (2 Sam. 21:15). The New International Bible says that David "grew exhausted."

The original Hebrew word for "wax faint" may not be important. But consider the English word *exhaust* often used to define an automobile tailpipe. An exhaust is that place where the fumes are expelled after the fuel is all used up. According to Dr. E. J. Kepler, "In the main, chronic fatigue is a disease of the intelligentsia. Doctors, lawyers, ministers and their wives, artists, musicians, students, teachers, big and little businessmen, executives, and white collar workers all grow exceedingly weary. Numbskulls rarely are affected."[9]

Stress and exhaustion use our years. And as the years go on, we find ourselves becoming increasingly more exhausted. We must learn how to overcome exhaustion by a flexible, ongoing program of delegation. In midlife, David was to find he couldn't defeat every giant. But he also found giant killing could be delegated. Of course, he wouldn't get the publicity he had received when he alone killed Goliath. But the organization could go on winning if he could give up his need to read his name in the papers.

Abishai, a part of his life team support group, suggested to David, "Thou shalt go no more out with us to battle, that thou quench not the light of Israel" (2 Sam. 21:17, KJV). What I think Abishai was really saying is, "Look, David, you're over fifty. You're old enough for an AARP card! Put your old fatigues in the national archives. Silver plate your old sword and hang it over your fireplace. Play a little more golf and try to keep the board of directors happy. Above all, quit trying to fight every battle by yourself. This company is no longer a one-man band; neither is this war. You must learn to delegate or get killed."

Abishai could see that the giant was getting the best of David and quickly came to his rescue. Frankly, David probably did not like being rescued. Who does? The glory always attends the rescuer and never the rescuee. But Abishai made his point, "Look, David, you're past middle age. Take a little more Geritol! Stop off at the nineteenth hole once in a while. Leave the giants to those of us who still work out every day!"

David was probably nervous, "You won't tell anybody that I had to be rescued, will you, Abishai?"

"Of course, I will! But it doesn't matter. You're the king. You can stand to share the glory, David. This is a big organization now. In a big organization, everybody should get a chance to kill a giant every now and then. Give everybody a little press! Hey, big guy! Take it on the chin! Smile! Share the giants! You're still the honcho of this enterprise!"

Perhaps you feel that this whole dialogue is imaginary. Perhaps it is taking a little liberty with Abishai's statement, "Thou shalt not go out with us to battle, that thou quench not the light of Israel." Still, delegation is an imperative for aging executives. Paul, as an old man, in his final book would say this very clearly to Timothy, "Thou therefore, my son, be strong in the grace that is in Christ Jesus, and the things that thou hast heard of me among many witnesses, the same commit thou to faithful men, who shall be able to teach others also" (2 Tim. 2:1–2, KJV). What Paul was saying to Timothy was, "Learn to delegate."

Delegation is a hard truth for young pastors to learn. They want to be sure everything gets done. They develop a penchant for jumping into all kinds of ministry vacuums left by uncommitted laypersons. Doing everything themselves, they learn, is one way to be sure everything gets done.

The weekly church bulletin was the nemesis of my first years as a pastor. All through my early ministry, I did the weekly bulletin myself. I didn't need to print the bulletin to think well of myself. It was just that there was a short line of those those who came forward begging to do it. So much of all that needs to be done in churches is not served by a rich volley of volunteers. So I ran the mimeograph machine and duplicated the forms. After years and years of purple-handed preaching, I made a decision. If I were ever fortunate enough to get another church to pastor, I would never do bulletins. If the church thought them important, someone who thought they were important would have to do them. If not, no bulletins!

In my next church, I lived up to that pledge. Therein lay the discovery of a valuable truth. I call this rich bit of administration lore, "lay low and wait for a layman." Sometimes we only get the chance to delegate what we refuse to do. But may our small warfare with the laity teach us what David learned fighting giants: You may avoid exhaustion and fatigue if you learn to delegate.

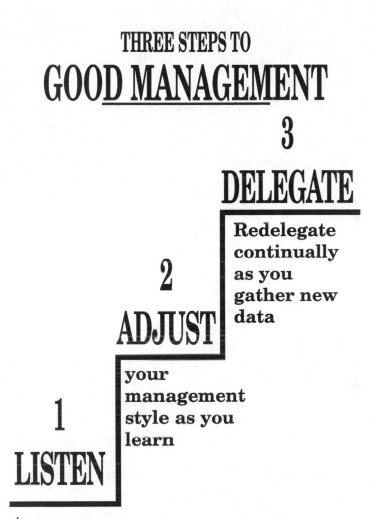

THREE STEPS TO
GOOD MANAGEMENT

3

DELEGATE

Redelegate continually as you gather new data

2

ADJUST

your management style as you learn

1

LISTEN

to everyone

Listen, Adjust Your Management Style, and Then Delegate

In small organizations, great ideas can come from anyone. But in large organizations, ideas tend to flow from the top down. But in 2 Samuel 21:17 David showed us how important it is to listen to underlings. The key thing he showed us is that you will never hear from underlings as long as you tend to see them that way. David heard from Abishai because he saw him as a friend and advisor and not as a subordinate.

Notice that a progression unfolds here. First, David hears. Then he adjusts his management style. Last of all, he takes Abishai's advice and delegates all future giant killing to the proper committee. Great leaders are frequently plagued by an obscene rationale. They tend to get older and weaker as their organizations get larger and more demanding. These leaders face one of two options: They will either frazzle out, and in time perhaps be kicked out. Or they will get smart and delegate. The process of getting smart means that they must turn their ear downward in the organization.

Those who listen down set themselves up for a glorious era of old-age veneration. Downward-listening leaders endear themselves to people who love their boss for really listening to them. Did Abishai venerate David in such a manner? I suspect that often, in his golden years, he stopped by David's tomb, laid a wreath on it, and exulted, "This man was truly a man for all seasons." All leaders gain esteem by listening downward.

Great Leaders Delegate the Task, and Then Share the Publicity

It is a sin for pastors to delegate the church's work to laypeople, yet horde the glory of lay achievement for themselves. As we have said, great leaders delegate tasks and give all the glory of achievement to those who did the work.

Let us return for a moment to the horrible giant Ishbi-Benob, who proved to be too much a match for David. David may have slashed the giant's knees a couple of times before he realized that this giant was really too much for him. The issue of his last birthday may have raised a grim spectre before him. Were the giants getting taller or was he losing his grip on life? Arthur laments in *Camelot* that every year his horse got "higher." David found himself in this lamentable predicament.

David hated to give up this kind of outing. Giant killing is the last thing leaders hate to surrender. It is here that they fly the flags. Frankly, it seems a kind of admission that we are getting old. It insinuates that we are moving from living to reverie. We who once did it are but leafing through scrapbooks of old headlines. But worst of all, to give up giant killing is to surrender the joy and celebration of the event. It says, "You're through in the big arena. You may toss out the ball that starts the World Series, but you will never stand on the mound in a uniform again. Your game is over."

Great leaders can stand that. Still the game is easier for some to give up than the accolades. Remember that in David's earlier life the great cry on the way back from the valley of Elah was, "Saul has slain his thousands and David his tens of thousands" (1 Sam. 18:7, KJV). There, in his macho youth, David learned how pleasing it is to slay giants and get the credit. Now Ishbi-Benob is killed, but Abishai gets the music and dancing. The people have a new giant killer! They sing that old song now full of discord. On the way home from the old men's wars, David must listen to them sing that jangling litany that once made Saul despise him: "David has slain his thousands, but Abishai his tens of thousands!"

But did David send Abishai a thank you card? The Bible is silent on this matter, but I have the feeling that he did. Why? Because I like to think that a man deep enough to write the Psalms would, in his later years, be wise enough to delegate the celebrated jobs.

Conclusion

Flexibility in management style speaks volumes to the leader's spiritual maturity. When a real leader uses the word *conversion,* he or she is not merely speaking of coming to Christ. Real leaders are daily being converted to new ways of doing things. Who can escape the truth of the doctrine breathed by Ebenezer Scrooge on Christmas morning? Remember how wisely he confesses, "I have a chance to change, and I will not be the man I was!" This continual confession is the daily life of the delegating, flexible leader.

The real process of change in our leadership style allows the mind a daily renewal. Paul wrote this outstanding counsel in Romans 12:2: "Be not conformed to this world, but be ye [continually] transformed by the [continual] renewing of your minds" (KJV). Admittedly, the bracketed words in the previous sentence are mine. However, they are not out of sync with a proper understanding of the Greek text. The person who is daily being converted to new ideas, adjusting the management style, and delegating is a leader. Such leaders cannot help but grow a company of people whose self-image is so strong it infuses the corporate image with power.

A dying dinosaur, in one of my children's books, offered Tommy this wise bit of counsel:

> Look at me, Tom. I'm the first of my kind.
> Take charge of your life, Pal. You must change to find
> All living is changing, begin with your mind!

> —from *Tommy and the Dinosaur*

Surviving a Visible Mistake

I wish that there were some wonderful place
Called the Land of Beginning Again,
Where all our mistakes and all our heartaches,
And all of our poor selfish grief
Could be dropped like a shabby old coat at the door
And never put on again.

Louise Fletcher Tarkington,
"The Land of Beginning Again"

I bargained with Life for a penny,
And Life would pay no more,
However I begged at evening
When I counted my scanty store.
For Life is a just employer,
He gives you what you ask,
But once you have set the wages,
Why, you must bear the task.
I worked for a menial's hire,
Only to learn, dismayed,
That any wage I had asked of Life,
Life would have paid.

Jessie B. Rittenhouse,
"My Wage"

I'm too big to cry and it hurts too much to laugh.

An American presidential candidate,
upon losing the election

Letter 10

Dear Leader:

I don't know if you heard about the preacher down in Payton County. He had one of them consolidated country churches containing about an equal number of Episcopalians, Presbyterians, and Baptists. Well, he took the Sunday offering and ran off with his secretary and went dancing. Just as you'd suspect, he got fired. The Episcopalians couldn't forgive him for stealing the offering. The Presbyterians couldn't forgive him for running off with the church secretary. And the Baptists couldn't forgive him for dancing. But, you know, those Unitarians forgave him for all three things. They even hired him as their preacher. He turned out to be the best pastor they ever had.

The man turned out fine. Ever after that he lived a life decent enough to keep the Unitarians happy. It just goes to show you that sometimes, if you forgive a man his mistakes, he can actually turn out to do a large amount of good in the world.

Well, Pastor, I just heard that you made a mistake—not bad enough, mind you, to hand you over to the Unitarians, but bad. I don't know why you did it, but some people here feel you oughta be fired. Not me. I think people should be forgiven for their mistakes as long as they're not great big mistakes and they don't do it very often and it's no skin off my nose.

Personally I have always felt that an honest mistake shows two things. First of all, the mistaker was doing something. The only people who never do anything wrong usually never do anything, period. But second, every mistake is a learning experience. Everybody who makes one learns one more thing that just shouldn't be done. Besides, Jesus said, "Blessed are the merciful for they shall obtain mercy" (Matt. 5:7, KJV). I'm turning thumbs up on you in case I someday do something stupid and have to look to you for a little understanding.

So, regarding the mistake you just made, I completely forgive you. It wasn't nearly as bad as that Unitarian preacher down in Payton County. Frankly, I don't see what the big deal is. Since you didn't abscond with the church funds and take your secretary dancing, I don't see why the Episcopalians and Presbyterians and Baptists can't all line up on your side too.

—Your Follower

2 Samuel 11:16–26; Psalm 51:4,12–14

No great life has ever been lived without pain.

David had celebrated a progression of victories and national successes. The acclaim of these successes may have caused the king to take moral liberties. When we receive much acclaim, it is sometimes easy to excuse our indiscretions. Perhaps David's rise to power brought him to this point.

David's survival of his affair with Bathsheba shows that great leaders can indeed transcend their mistakes. I believe survival is best achieved when three factors enter into play: openness, forgiveness of others, and a recognition that we are all in the process of maturing.

Openness is an imperative quality in a leader's life. Those who can live in openness best survive their mistakes. Crises such as Watergate make it clear that all of us are more tolerant of admitted mistakes than false denials. In King David's case, he did for a while try to cover up his affair. His murder of Uriah and his duplicity with Nathan the prophet could not long be hidden. What is admirable is that once he was discovered, David openly declared that he was not above reproach. Kings can be guilty of sin. Psalm 51 is a public acknowledgment of David's need for repentance.

The second quality a leader must cultivate is a spirit of forgiveness. All sin from time to time. The story of David illustrates that it is good for us to forgive others just in case we someday need them to return the favor. There is an old Sanskrit saying that reads:

> The anger of a good man
> lasts an instant;
> that of a meddler two hours;
> that of a base man a day and a night;
> and that of a great sinner until death.[1]

Forgiving others is not just medicine you give them; forgiveness is the tonic you take yourself. If you do not drink deeply of the forgiveness you extend, your grudges will in

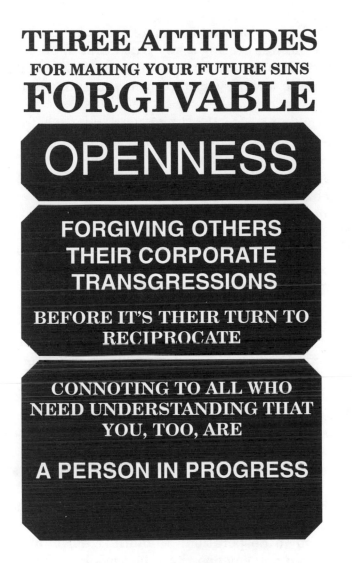

THREE ATTITUDES
FOR MAKING YOUR FUTURE SINS
FORGIVABLE

OPENNESS

**FORGIVING OTHERS
THEIR CORPORATE
TRANSGRESSIONS**

**BEFORE IT'S THEIR TURN TO
RECIPROCATE**

**CONNOTING TO ALL WHO
NEED UNDERSTANDING THAT
YOU, TOO, ARE**

A PERSON IN PROGRESS

time poison your soul. Your leadership will be crippled at last by a narrow, stingy humanity. Eugene Habecker advises us: "A leader who has not learned to be a good forgiver will not be as effective as one who has. Leadership affords too many uncomfortable incidents, too many inaccurate accusations, and too little time to keep track of everyone who has 'wronged' you."[2] Jesus said, "In everything, do to others what you would have them do to you"

(Matt. 7:12, NIV). He was not merely stating a nice principle of life. He was stating a key truth that applies to every arena of leadership. A follower you treat with charity is far more prone to forgive you when you yourself are caught in a storm of contempt.

Jesus told a parable about a steward who was forgiven a great debt. However, in the wake of his forgiveness he became hard and unforgiving. To demand, "Pay back what you owe me!" (Matt. 18:28, NIV) is hardly defensible after a great debt has been forgiven. In His model prayer, Jesus taught us to pray, "Forgive us our debts as we also have forgiven our debtors" (Matt. 6:12, NIV). Such a prayer lies at the heart of surviving a mistake. If your followers see your charity in a moment of their great need, they will softly lay aside a gift of mercy for your future need.

There is one final quality you should develop to save your future with forgiveness. You must communicate to people that you are a fallible human being. Like all the world around you, you are a person in process. Process people are much easier to forgive when they are caught in error than those who try to project that they are perfectly finished and full of wisdom. The right to mature is bought with our humanity.

You can establish the idea that you are a person in process by doing a few very simple things. Let others see you goof up. Let those around you see you change your mind from time to time. Let others see you do things differently than you did yesterday. One of Gandhi's disciples once confronted him in desperation: "Gandhi, I don't understand you. How can you say one thing last week, and something quite different this week?"

"Ah," Gandhi replied, "because I have learned something since last week."

David lived with his best warriors for a long time. David's close proximity to his men may have allowed them to see him as a person in process. In his close living with these men he had avoided a cold, professional remoteness. Doubtlessly David had a forgiving spirit as well. Without these qualities, the Bathsheba affair would have destroyed him.

It is rare for an indulgent soul to grant itself only one liberty. Usually a granted liberty becomes the foundation of a future license. After having sent the army out to do battle rather than leading it, David became easy prey to sexual indulgence (see 2 Sam. 11:2–5).

After Bathsheba became pregnant, the king tried to protect himself from scandal. First he tried the cover-up approach. Then, under pressure, he openly dealt with the problem. Within the context of Christian ministry, some mistakes are more forgivable than others. Mistakes in judgment, I believe, can generally be forgiven. On the other hand, mistakes involving immorality are not so easily forgiven, particularly in the more conservative denominations. But whether any mistake is forgiven depends upon the approach that the leader takes in seeking reconciliation. There really are only two approaches that can be taken. The first is the cover-up approach, in which case a congregation must discover the sin. This approach is somehow hardest to forgive. The second approach is the openness approach. This confessional bridge is self-revelatory. It is much easier to forgive.

The Cover-Up

The cover-up approach is totally ego-defensive. It is based on the false idea that "people will think less of me if they really know what I am or what I have done." However, the real truth is that people can accept weaknesses more readily than hypocrisy. David's hypocrisy appeared in his attempt to fool his friend Uriah (see 2 Sam. 17). Cover-up usually attempts to bypass God's requirement of repentance. While we cover up our sins, we usually are failing to seek the forgiveness of God. The sin of failing to seek repentance is the real unforgivable sin. This smug, self-satisfied hypocrisy feels little need of reaching out to God.

Usually, when we don't beg forgiveness from those we hurt, we don't seek God's forgiveness either.

Genuine confession begins in the free admission that, when we hurt others, we really hurt God. God loves everyone. So passionate is that love that our very injuries become the wounds of God. So our unacknowledged wrongs against others leave great gaps in our relationship with our heavenly Father.

Whenever parents watch their children quarrel, it stabs the heart of the parents. It is not just that quarreling children wrong each other, they wrong the parents who gave them life. Yet quarreling children are usually so possessed of their own agenda that they rarely look beyond their selfish positions to see that they are actually hurting their parents. It is usually only after the children have asked each other's forgiveness that they turn to see their parents. There they stand broken and waiting in the wings for their reconciliation.

Covering up bad relationships indicates that a leader has not dealt with the heavenly dimensions of his or her problems. Let us not forget that in Christian leadership we are really talking about servant leadership. This dimension implies that the servant is waiting on God primarily. Cover-up wounds the process. It introduces such a distance between the king and the servant that the way back to relationship becomes a severe ascent. But how does it all get going? What is the process that ends up killing both our lateral relationship with our peers and our more important vertical relationship with God? It all has to do with ego and image.

Serving the Ego vs. Serving the People

Twice in the story at hand, David tried to get his friend Uriah to sleep with Bathsheba. David's child would then appear to be Uriah's son. What rationale did David use to justify his deception? I think his reasoning was split on the issue. First, national esteem and adulation had gone to his head. It is difficult when swimming in a sea of compliments to get a real picture of who we really are. When we reach that ultimate plateau when everyone thinks well of us, we begin to join our fans in their idolatry. At this state we lose objectivity. We begin to see ourselves as a god. Our rise to membership in the Trinity blurs our view of reality. We come to believe we have a right to own whatever we want to own. David had everything, what was one wife more? He was, after all, a god! How opposite is this attitude from that of the Lord Jesus. Listen to the words of John Haggai:

> Jesus Christ, the ultimate example of leadership, lived a life of humility. The Lord of earth and heaven dressed in a garb of rustic! He who poured out the waters of the earth—the Amazon, the Euphrates, the Nile, the Mississippi—bent over a well to ask a Samaritan woman for a drink. He who spread the canopy of the heavens and set the earth for a footstool, spent the night with Simon a tanner. He whose chariots are the clouds, walked with sore feet.[3]

I have come to believe that many of the nationally known evangelists believe themselves invincible. Some of their ministries collapsed around the loss of their moral consciences. This may have been due to the "godhood syndrome." Having achieved a kind of lesser godhood, they opted for greater godhood. All that they wanted, they had. If they did not have it, they could get it by selling an airplane or hyping their appeals. They found it easier to forgive themselves for the illicit when their disciples by their compliments granted them superstar status. Having been given all that can be had legitimately, they then seize what can only be had illegitimately.

James Thurber told a tale about an owl who thought he was a god. This owl was asked some simple questions by various forest creatures. They asked him, for instance, to give them a sound, interrogative pronoun. "Whoooooo!" replied the owl. The animals were amazed at his erudition. One creature held up two fingers and then asked this owl how many fingers she was holding up. "Twoooo!" said the owl. The creatures broke into applause. At last one of them asked why a lover called on his love. The owl replied "to Woooo!" It was glorious. The owl was a leader and a genius. The forest creatures began to cry in one voice that he was God. With their applause, the owl began to gain arrogance. They coaxed him down from the tree and put him out front of his growing crowd of supporters. He led them in an arrogant kind of triumphal march.

Marching was all rather hard for Owl, a natural tree dweller and sometimes flyer. But when the compliments are coming fast, and everybody is shouting, "He's God! He's God!" it gets hard to remember what your real weaknesses are. Owl also did not see very well in the light, which made his daytime leadership precarious. Blinking and squinting and trying to see the course his leadership should take, Owl led his adoring supporters out onto a busy highway. There they were all run over by a sixteen-wheeler. This ended their support for a leader of brief divinity. The highway was scattered with their soft, furry forms. Here was an evidence that it is dangerous for a leader to allow his constituency to overcompliment him. He was led into assumptions he couldn't handle. David, like Owl, may have been flattered into a view of himself that told him there was nothing off limits to his advancing ego.

The second snare in David's thinking had to do with a most basic kind of sin, the sin against human dignity. This sin falsely believes that some individuals have greater worth to God than others. God detests this horrible sin because it allows us to devalue souls. Once we devalue others, we treat them in ways that are demeaning. Such devaluation relegates human beings to chattel. Then they can be used or destroyed as we will. Uriah was a Gentile. In a Jewish nation, David felt that he would not be a great loss. Uriah was expendable. How would the world be affected if it were somehow one Gentile short?

This statement is much akin to Scrooge's comment. When asked for a donation at Christmas, Scrooge turned to the community do-gooders and asked, "Are there no workhouses for the poor to go to?" When told that many of the poor would rather die than go there, again he crassly replied, "Well, if they would rather die, perhaps they had better do so and decrease the surplus population." There is no sin worse than seeing real live souls and considering them either "surplus" or "expendable." The world, as David saw it, could get along without another Gentile. After all, it would not be quite the same to mistreat (or even murder) a Gentile as it would to do so to one of God's chosen people. In this story we hear God saying, "All people are my people, and everybody is worth exactly the same to me whether they be kings or mercenaries."

When covering up our mistakes, it is easy to sacrifice other people to keep from blemishing our own reputation.

Stop-Gapping God's Spirit

It is not just that David used Uriah; it was that his use was demeaning. He got Uriah drunk (to make it easier to send him home) so that he might be enticed to sleep with Bathsheba. In such a drunken stupor, Uriah would not clearly recall whether he had slept with Bathsheba. All of this was done so that David could foster the notion within Uriah that the unborn child was his own. It was not what this chicanery did to Uriah that mattered before God. Uriah did not lose his dignity. It was David who lost status before God. God's influence in the king's life was gone. In the Psalms David had written much about the power of the indwelling Spirit. Now in his willful abuse of a trusted friend, he had stop-gapped the Spirit of God.

In my book *The Valiant Papers,* I suggest that Satan fell out of favor with God by taking liberty from his disciplined necessity of praise. Satan began his fall by skipping his "morning alleluias." David's plunge into sin did not begin just by watching Bathsheba take a bath. It really began by taking little liberties. He stayed home at a time when kings go forth to battle (see 2 Sam. 11:1–3). As a powerful leader, he began to demand less of himself than he did of his followers. David, because he was a king, excused his lack of discipline. He somehow felt that it would be all right to let others do the fighting while he slept late. He would use Saturday morning for his own agendas. But does the passage imply even more? Did David also take some liberties with his spiritual disciplines as well? Did he skip his morning alleluias?

We who lead are always accountable for our morning alleluiahs. When we begin to "sleep in," we too begin our own fall. Sooner or later we sleep through our important meeting times with God. All spiritual accountability is lost. It is a great moment in the fifty-first Psalm when David at last acknowledged, "Against thee, thee only have I sinned" (Psalm 51:4, KJV). With this admission, David's split soul turns back to God. Psalm 51 shouts this one great truth: Our primary sins are never against those we wrong. Our primary sins are against God.

Charles Spurgeon commented concerning this verse: "The virus of sin lies in its opposition to lead: the psalmist's sense of sin towards others rather tended to increase the force of the feeling of sin against God. All his wrongdoing centered, culminated, and came to a climax at the foot of the divine throne. To injure our fellow men is sin, mainly because in doing so we violate the law of God."[4] The source of our sins is never our grand offenses (like demeaning and murdering Uriah). Sins take root in our tiny permissions— our neglect (like skipping our quiet times).

Did David's sin against God and Uriah mean that he had completely quit his seasons of prayer? I doubt it. We who believe are an odd mixture of sin and supplication. I do not believe that the fallen evangelists of the 1980s ever ceased their praying. They were talking to God even as they fell. They obviously continued praying publicly, and I suspect that they continued their private devotion as well. But how could they? How could King David go on praying as he murdered and deceived? The same way we all do it. We compartmentalize our private agendas with a strong wall that keeps them separate from our devotional life. James speaks of double-mindedness:

> [H]e is a double-minded man, unstable in all he does. (Jas. 1:8, NIV)

> Come near to God and he will come near to you. Wash your hands, you sinners, and purify your hearts, you double-minded. (Jas. 4:8, NIV)

The word *double-minded* in the Greek is essentially a word that means "two-souled." David's continued devotional life, while he continually sinned, meant that he was double-minded. Double-mindedness is the practice of holding two conflicting, separate ideas in our minds at the same time. We sin by accepting them both. Thus, we allow Christ to indwell our lives even as we continue to pursue our self-interest.

David's complex scheme to do away with Uriah required an involved complicity in the lives of many others. Not that this was altogether surprising, for sin has a spreading system of tentacles that ultimately involves everyone. It is not David the human being who surprises us. It is David the writer of Psalms who leaves us aghast.

In an elaborate act of scheming, David goes national with his deception. In the first part of 2 Samuel 11, David wanted Uriah and Bathsheba to appear happily married. Later David decided to take Uriah's wife, thus deceiving the whole nation. In this act, the king's cover-up became complex. David's crime became a stain on his servant leadership and the nation's image. More than that, it was a flippant proclamation that morality doesn't much matter if you hold the power. David's Libertinism shouted, "My power is my entitlement." Those who hold power are often God enough to forgive themselves.

Ending Cover-Up: Self-Protection Yielding to Self-Surrender

Cover-up is a face-saving device designed to protect our reputation. Those who resort to it opt for saving their image, usually at the price of losing their authenticity.

There is only one way out of this egocentric deception. We must return to the source of all spiritual vitality—surrender. Such surrender grows for the leader, as it does for the follower, out of the double taproot of Galatians 2:20. We must be crucified with Christ to live meaningfully. We must take from Galatians 2:20 and Romans 6:11 and reckon ourselves dead. Then our demanding self-image can gradually lose its power over us. Paul dealt very seriously with his aggressive ego. So must we. Our esteemed Dr. Jeckyll must always rebuke our foul usurper, the warped Mr. Hyde. When our old sin nature is once again in submission, sooner or later our servanthood will bring us kneeling into God's presence.

I remember that during our final and financially demanding building program, I was barely able at times to remember that we were collecting funds to build a church house and not a monument. The crowds had become unmanageable in our old facility. Those times when the church most needed a new building were also those times when I was most widely celebrated for the numerical success of the church. How much life's little successes lead us to celebrate ourselves!

I could only uphold my porcelain ego by indulging in Christian relativism. I was somewhat successful if I compared myself with bigger losers than I was. But I shied away from comparing myself with all those who were building multi-million dollar buildings in exotic Disney World motifs.

If we want to celebrate our own walk in Christ, we must never compare ourself to Mother Theresa, only Al Capone. Of course, then we can really feel ourselves truly spiritual. I had a $4-million building program going. Thus I could not compare my own achievement with those megachurch icons who were building $30-million worship centers. In such carnal relativism, I could remain swaggering and boastful over my little achievements.

It is important to our spiritual maturity to celebrate those who outsucceed us. Tragically I see very little of this. In any given city there is often fierce jealousy and competition raging among pastors who serve within the same city limits. Most of these would celebrate Christ in the same way. But double-mindedness keeps their piety and honesty in opposite pockets. They rarely call their egos to yield in congratulating a succeeding brother. They only seem to advance by lobbying for a continual celebration of themselves. Year after year, such persons may preach the sweetness of grace yet they live out a never-ending war of suspicion and gossip. Thus they may keep an aura of spiritual submission while they build shrines of self-importance.

Nothing serves our egos quite so much as our officialness at our particular shrine. We who lead are the keepers of those shrines. I remember a board meeting of our association. Two churches that had struggled for years were fighting losing battles to stay alive in a downtown area of the city. Their congregations were being transported to their churches in vans and busses. Everybody in both situations was being bussed. One of them had a fair crowd but no building. The other had a fair building but no crowd. I made a motion that the two be joined into one church. Putting two incomes together in one church would allow them to sell one building. Then they would have enough extra income to purchase a large facility and have a church secretary, which neither of the churches had ever been able to afford. One pastor thought the merger would be a great idea and would provide badly needed space for both of them. I remember watching the other pastor vigorously protest this possible merger. He could not bear to lose control of his shrine. At this writing, the two very small churches (each has less than thirty in attendance) still own their own real estate and still struggle with minimal funds and dead opportunities.

It is difficult to rebuke egocentric leadership. The disease affects us all. But it is not hard at all to prescribe the cure. The cure lies in surrender. G. K. Chesterton pictured Francis of Assisi breaking with his father's dreams. Francis would never take over the family business as his father hoped. The young Francis was not free to serve himself. He had been bought with a price (see 1 Cor. 6:20). After this sublimation of his life to Christ, things financial lost their hold on him. How submissive was Francis? Well, they say he had a custom of kissing lepers in ordinary greeting. Kissing lepers is only for those who have given so much away that they have nothing else to lose.

Christian leaders who really move their world are not generally conscious of their self-surrender. Yielding to Christ has become so much a part of them that they no longer see anything remarkable in it. One of my favorite missionaries is Rebecca Naylor. I really don't know her personally as well as I would like. I have had the privilege of shaking her hand only a time or two. She is not self-serving. She seems to need no accolades to serve. My awe of all that she is as a Christian leader would dumbfound her. The fact that she is generally considered to be a brilliant physician does not distract her servanthood. Her years of service in the hospital at Bangalore, India, have spawned over four hundred local Indian congregations. These churches have grown directly out of her yieldedness to the church and the people of India. I perceive her with fascination. She makes no attempt to be humble. For her, that would imply a kind of pride. She refuses to foster any image for others to celebrate. She certainly makes no attempt to celebrate herself. What does she do? She simply walks her yielded way with Christ. Let others assess, complain, or celebrate. There is work to be done. There is a God to be served.

Cover-up is a kind of sickness for those who forget that their careers have significance to God alone. To be successful is to be obedient. Great leaders want only this yielded definition of success. "Besides," said Jesus, "What doth it profit a man if he becomes a CEO and loses his relationship with God" (see Luke 9:25)? Lord, teach all of us who lead to pray this simple prayer, "God, may my double-mindedness fade to single issue: 'for me to live is Christ' (Phil. 1:21). Then, Father, my leadership will know no duplicity of image, for there will be nothing to cover up." In this new single-mindedness we will walk lockstepped with Kierkegaard's truth, "Purity of heart is to will one thing."

The Openness Approach: Psalm 51:4,12–14

No one expects a flawed leader to lead flawlessly. But everyone, even people whose lives are flawed, expect moral leadership. If we are guilty of anything morally compromising, we must quickly become overt rather than covert in dealing with our trespasses We should openly acknowledge our failures. Our failures teach us our need for God. God remains our Father even when we lose. Sid Lovett prayed the "Loser's Prayer" at the annual Kodak banquet gathered to select the coach of the year. "Thou art a God of mercy and so we lift before Thy care those coaches, who with endurance and honor but a losing record, are grateful for a new year. Deliver them from the nightmares of instant replay and sullen alumni. And if it please Thee, bestow upon them surefingered ends, fleet runners with secure cartilages, and linemen of granite."[5]

To be human is to be open about our humanity. We all lose, but all losers begin to look like winners the moment they become open about losing. Sadly, in David's case, his openness turned out to be an induced openness. The prophet Nathan used a bit of narrative theology (see 2 Sam. 12:1–7) to force the king's acknowledgment of his sins. Sooner or later our sins find us out. So it is best to be openly confessional.

When the leader covers up, the church is informed by covert gossip and innuendo. The leader's sins become less forgivable than when the leader bares his soul voluntarily. Psalm 51 is the record of David's coming out of the closet. His openness began where it ought, with God. It is clear from the story that he was forced—probably by a blitz of gossip—to acknowledge his sin. Gossip is viciously explosive. People in the nineteenth century had a way of saying that collecting and correcting a blitz of gossip was like trying to collect all the feathers from a ruptured pillow and put them back into the casing. So David's expensive affair cannot ever be neatly packaged. Sin is never neatly packaged stuff.

If we pull the sin over into the realm of family relationships, the principle is easily understood. What wife would not prefer to hear from her own husband any tale of his complicity. How sad to hear it from a gossipy circle of informers. No forced openness holds the power of reconciliation, like spontaneous confession.

The curative process for our moral mistakes can bring healing only in this three-step process. The first step is acknowledging our hypocrisy. The second is repentance. The third is the restoration of praise.

Step One: Acknowledging Our Hypocrisy

Which of us who lived through Watergate will ever forget its horrible end? We mentioned the scandal at the beginning of this chapter. I will forever see, in my mind's eye, Richard Nixon. Under threat of impeachment, he walked that hideous red carpet to mount the helicopter. He didn't just leave the White House, but the presidency of the United States. How haggard his steps! How visible the rounding of his shoulders! How obvious his downcast eyes! How humiliated his family! How shredded his dignity! One thing that had caused this sad spectacle: cover-up. He failed to acknowledge his hypocrisy. Many historians and

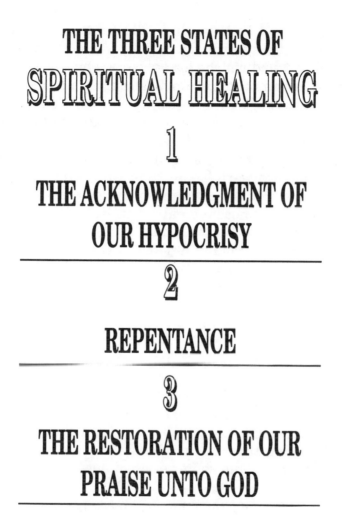

THE THREE STATES OF
SPIRITUAL HEALING

1
THE ACKNOWLEDGMENT OF OUR HYPOCRISY

2
REPENTANCE

3
THE RESTORATION OF OUR PRAISE UNTO GOD

political analysts feel that if the President had spontaneously acknowledged his sin, his sins might all have been forgiven. But protesting his innocence while the unfolding evidence indicated his complicity, was at last unforgivable.

David's acknowledgment came later. But in Psalm 51:4 he confessed that his primary offense was not against Bathsheba or Uriah or Israel. The worst kind of complicity is spiritual rather than political. Why? Perhaps because in the minds of most people, spiritual hypocrisy makes God look bad. At least Richard Nixon did not try to appear spiritually pure. One can imagine how we would have felt if the President had called repeatedly on the name of Christ to protest his innocence. Somehow a contemptible hostility is born out of spiritual hypocrisy.

If we are prone to doubt this, one can feel it in the case of those evangelists who fell from public esteem in the eighties. A great many bawdy and cheap jokes were made about Bakker and Swaggart—more than were ever made about Nixon. There was a heavy national remorse for a fallen President. We did not laugh about it. But with the evangelists we did laugh. For the most part, we deal with religious hypocrisy by poking fun at it. I think that we do this to get God off the hook. By laughing at the faultiness of religious hypocrites, we believe we somehow save the holiness of God.

David's repentance was written in much pain (see Ps. 51:12). The real price we pay for our hypocrisy is lost joy. But the pain is always a healer. When our brokenness is splinted with the pain of our confession, then healing can begin. Our son on one occasion suffered a broken arm. The doctor set the arm, and it continued to mend for several weeks. Then the doctor called us in for a second set of X-rays. Following those X-rays he said to us, "I have some good news for you and some very bad news."

"Let's have the good news first," I begged.

"Well," said the doctor, "the good news is the arm is healing very fast. The bad news is that it is not healing straight. We are going to have to break it—with your permission, of course—and reset it."

Reluctantly I agreed. I had no idea how he rebroke the bone. I could barely stand the thought of this huge physician intentionally breaking my son's arm. How would he do it? Would he take the tiny arm in his huge, hairy, freckled hands and physically snap it over his knee like cordwood? I didn't like the pain of thinking about it. Still, I knew that the ultimate healing of my child somehow laid in this difficult process of brokenness.

"Make me to hear joy and gladness," cries David, "that the bones which you have broken may rejoice" (Ps. 51:8, NKJV). Only after God took David's soul in His God-sized hands and snapped it in pain, could healing properly begin. But make no mistake about it, hypocrisy never heals straight. It is brittle. The jagged break it makes is compound in any life. Ask Richard Nixon. Still the hypocrisy must be acknowledged before the healing can begin. My son's arm would be crooked even now in his manhood, except for my long-ago permission. Hypocrisy ends where brokenness permits its healing.

Step Two: Coming to Repentance

Repentance is not telling God what we have done wrong. God could scarcely be God and need us to inform Him on any subject.

Repentance has a single aim: the restoration of relationship. God knows the exact nature of our sins and their effects on our lives. Since we cannot enlighten God's understanding of our sins, why bring them up at all? Because every unconfessed sin adds another brick on a wall of our broken relationships. Ultimately that wall will separate us from Him. Repentance, on the other hand, obliterates that wall and makes us one. Repentance is not informing God about our morality. It is a heart cry of acknowledgment. It is crying over the awful distance that has come to separate us from Him.

Consider the realm of marital relationships. When mates offend each other, each knows the other's transgression. How shall such marriages be restored? The question is not one of telling each other what they have done wrong. The rupture will heal around marital repentance. Someone must say: "I'm sorry. I agree that I have done wrong. I ask you to forgive me. I want every wall in our relationship to come down."

For every leader the same principle holds true. A congregation may feel that the pastor is covering up some sin. Still, there is no chance of healing until the wrong is acknowledged and the relationship restored. Repentance is a threefold process. First, we survey our wrong. Second, we admit the error. Finally, we seek a restoration of joy.

Step Three: The Restoration of Praise

After his sin, David promised to teach transgressors to praise God (see Ps. 51:12–15). Praise, at its ultimate, forsakes its intrigue with failure. It wakens within us an intense focus on God and His glory.

Praise moves the focus from our pain to the person and work of Jesus Christ. Praise is immensely liberating because it gets our minds off ourselves. Glorifying God pulls our mired souls from the slough of failure, and we really are positively free.

Conclusion

Praise serves even greater ends than freeing us from enslavement. It opens us up. When the elation of praise takes hold, our loss of inhibition is glorious. Consider the secular aspect of this for a moment. In close athletic contests the souls of the coach, players, team, and audience become fused in intensity. The euphoria of praising the team fills the arena before them. At such moments their behavior is barely sane. When the game is well fought, the madness, the mood, and the exaggerated behavior of the crowd leads all to deserve the word *fan,* which is short for *fanatic.* In the afterglow of such moments, the elation itself tells us that praise is liberating. The heaviness of the psalmist in Psalm 51 moved to sheer lightness of being. One of the great gifts that leaders can give to those they lead is an unashamed need to praise. This must exist first in the pastor and then in the followers. Thus is the whole congregation set free.

George Truett, long-time pastor of the First Baptist Church of Dallas, once went hunting with his friend, the sheriff of Dallas County. During the expedition, Dr. Truett accidentally shot and killed his friend. It was a costly, horrible mistake. Dr. Truett's soul was all but destroyed because of the accident. It was his intention never to preach again. But, bit by bit, the affirmation of God healed and convinced him that God must yet be served. The most grievous mistakes of our lives should never be allowed to cast us away unused. Dr. Truett became one of the greatest preachers and pastors in Christian history.

Are pastors to be forgiven any more readily than others? No, but neither are they to be judged more severely. Pastors are leaders whose temptations are immense. In some ways the counseling pressures laid on them sets them up for moral compromise. They do not often fall. When they do, a kind of Christian charity ought to keep the unfallen redeemed from shooting their wounded. They, like laypersons, can never be excused for licenses they grant themselves. But overly harsh judgment from either pastors or laity cannot be condoned. Paul, warning us against such a spirit, once said, "Let him who thinks he stands take heed, lest he fall" (1 Cor. 10:12, KJV). An unthinkable severity prompts unforgiving spirits. Such Christians, in an earlier time, would have picked up stones against the poor woman in John 8. Jesus' invitation was, "Let him who is without sin among you be the first to cast a stone at her" (John 8:7, AMP). Eugene Habecker puts it all into perspective: "Does the leader (and others for that matter) have to be forgiven 'bad' sins? The obvious inference here is that there are 'good' sins, which are not worthy of significant organizational response and which can be forgiven. And then there are 'bad' sins, which if committed by the leader or others, and even when forgiveness is extended, will almost surely result in dismissal."[6]

Two or three times in my life I have had a pastor friend who made a very visible mistake in his life. Each, in turn, confessed his sins to the church. Each then placed himself under the judgment of the church. Each yielded to the church's discipline. Each pastor agreed to counseling, and in time, was set free to begin pastoring once again.

One night my finest pastor friend called and, weeping on the other end of the phone, began to tell me of a sin in his life. "I have begged my wife to forgive me, and she has," he wept. "I have also asked God to forgive me, and He has. Now," he went on, "all that remains is for me to cast myself upon the counsel and mercy of my congregation. I trust that their compassion will at least be adequate to forgive me." I could genuinely weep with him. Even today as he pastors once again, I have come to know that the complete forgiveness of God is with him and this forgiveness holds within it his possibility for new use. Only a severely requiring church should ever remove a God-called person from all possibility of use.

David of Israel instructs us. Leaders can survive a visible mistake. Their leadership can survive it as well. I do not say this to encourage moral looseness. But let the church call her fallen to hope. Judges 16:21–22 records of Samson: "The Philistines took him and put out his eyes. . . . Howbeit, the hair of his head began to grow again" (KJV).

We preachers tend to measure our success in the number of Philistines we convert. Samson measured the success of his leadership totally in the number of dead Philistines. This may seem a bit morbid. Still, if you grant him the joy he found in killing Philistines, his triumph is remarkable. If you graph out the number of Philistines he slew, you must concede that Samson succeeded. Israel felt that his Philistine-killing was worthy of mention in the Scriptures. His last stand in the temple of Dagon was *Fortune* magazine stuff. Standing with his arms around the two middle pillars of the house, he prayed for a successful conclusion to his life.

Can a leader survive a visible mistake? The Scriptures testify, "So the dead which he slew at his death were more than those he slew in his life" (Judg. 16:30, KJV). Did God hear an old Nazarite who had slept with his enemy and corrupted himself with immoral drunkenness? See the titan Samson bend himself against the cold stone. The columns groan. His anguished soul begs God to hear him in spite of his old sins. "Oh Lord God, remember me. I pray Thee, and strengthen me. I pray Thee, only this once" (Judg. 16:28, KJV).

Samson does not survive his mistakes. He does serve God beyond his earlier failures. And he who was once set aside because of his sin is named once more a champion. Every leader has sometimes sought God's help and found God silent. But a worthy leader still trusts and decides in faith, even when God seems elusive.

Study the Bible as you study leadership. You will then stir morality into your leadership recipe. You will also find the Bible a wellspring of quietude. It will provide that depth of soul you need to stabilize the ups and downs of your leadership. The more the wisdom of Scripture pervades your views, the more those around you will trust you. Trust is the keen edge of the blade with which you sculpt all of life.

Lead only as you follow. If, as you look out ahead, you cannot see Christ, do not act. Never go it alone. Find yourself a wilderness of intention. Sit and beg His coming. When at last you feel His nearness, it will be time "to stand." The Bible summons all who would lead to stand.

> Wherefore take unto you the whole armor of God, that ye may be able to withstand in the evil day, and having done all, to stand. (Eph. 6:13, KJV)

> Stand fast therefore in the liberty by which Christ has made us free. (Gal. 5:1, NKJV)

> Stand fast in one spirit. (Phil. 1:27, NKJV)

> Stand fast in the Lord. (1 Thess. 3:8, NKJV)

Stand and lead. But never forget that we purchase the right to direct the church with the currency of our obedience. Therefore, speak only after you have listened. Lead only as you follow. Stand only after you have sat quietly in His presence. Raise your chin and command, only after you have bowed your head and obeyed.

Endnotes

Key 1

1. Mike Mason, *The Mystery of Marriage,* foreword by J. I. Packer (Portland: Multnomah Press, 1985), 37.

2. Friedrich Nietzsche, cited by John White, *Excellence in Leadership* (Downers Grove, Ill.: InterVarsity Press, 1986), 88.

3. Ibid., 89.

4. Max DePree, *Leadership Jazz* (New York: Doubleday, 1992), 222.

5. Stephen Covey, *The Seven Habits of Highly Effective People* (New York: Doubleday, 1992), 35.

6. J. Bronowski, *The Ascent of Man* (Boston: Little, Brown, and Assoc., 1973), 236.

7. Philip Greenslade, *Leadership, Greatness, and Servanthood* (Minnesota: Bethany House Publishers, 1984), 3–4.

8. Robert A. Raines, *Success Is a Moving Target* (Waco, Tex.: Word Books, 1975), 65.

9. Ibid.

10. Frank Nunlist, as quoted by Joe D. Batten, *Tough-Minded Management* (New York: AMACOM, 1963), 191–92.

Key 2

1. Peter I. Drucker, *Managing the Non-Profit Organization* (New York: Harper Business, 1990), 201.

2. Jean-Paul Sartre, *No Exit and Three Other Plays* (New York: Random House [Vintage Books], 1948), 77.

3. Stanley Coopersmith, *The Antecedents of Self-Esteem* (San Francisco: Freeman, 1967), 4–5.

4. Max DePree, *Leadership Jazz* (New York: Doubleday, 1992), 172–73.

5. A message as published in *The Wall Street Journal* by United Technologies Corporation, Hartford, Connecticut, cited in Warren Bennis and Burt Nanus, *Leaders: The Strategies for Taking Charge* (New York: Harper & Row, 1985), 22.

6. Warren Bennis, *Why Leaders Can't Lead* (San Francisco: Jossey-Bass Publishers, 1989), 50–51.

7. Jim Lundry, *Lead, Follow, or Get Out of the Way* (New York: Berkley Books, 1991), 84.

8. Wess Roberts, *Leadership Secrets of Attila the Hun* (Niles, Ill.: Nightingale-Conant Audio, 1989).

9. Lee Buck with Dick Schneider, *Tapping Your Secret Source of Power* (Old Tappan, N.J.: Revell, 1985), 144–45.

10. Drucker, 197.

11. Ibid., 196.

12. Ibid., 79.

13. Anthony Robbins, *Unlimited Power* (New York: Fawcett Columbine, 1986), 65.

14. Ibid., 375.

15. Joe D. Batten, *Tough-Minded Management* (New York: AMACOM, 1963), 176.

Key 3

1. Lee Buck, *Tapping Your Secret Source of Power* (Old Tappan, N.J.: Revell, 1985), 133.

2. Robert D. Dale, *Pastoral Leadership* (Nashville: Abingdon Press, 1986), 40ff.

3. Kenneth Blanchard, *The One Minute Manager* (New York: William Merrom and Company, Inc., 1985), 30.

4. Judith Viorst, *Necessary Losses* (New York: Simon & Schuster, 1986), 179–80.

5. Emilie Griffin, *Clinging* (San Francisco: Harper & Row, 1984), 43, citing Shakespeare, *Hamlet,* act 1, sc. 3, line 62.

6. Philip Greenslade, *Leadership, Greatness, and Servanthood* (Minnesota: Bethany House Publishers, 1984), 6.

7. Ibid., 70.

8. J. Paul Getty, *How to Be a Successful Executive* (New York: The Berkley Publishing Group, 1965), 92.

9. Max DePree, *Leadership Jazz* (New York: Doubleday, 1992), 66.

10. Buck, 134.

Key 4

1. Peter I. Drucker, *Managing the Non-Profit Organization* (New York: Harper Business, 1990), 40.

2. J. Paul Getty, *How to Be a Successful Executive* (New York: The Berkley Publishing Group, 1965), 123.

3. John Haggai, *Lead On!* (Waco, Tex.: Word Publishers, 1986), 12.

4. Quoted in Robert A. Raines, *Success Is a Moving Target* (Waco, Tex.: Word Books, 1975), 14.

5. Klaus Bockmuehl, *The Challenge of Marxism* (Downers Grove, Ill.: InterVarsity Press, 1980), 39.

6. Alan Loy McGinnis, *Bringing Out the Best in People* (Minneapolis: Augsburg Publishing House, 1985), 169.

7. Ralph W. Neighbour, Jr., *The Seven Last Words of the Church* (Nashville: Broadman Press, 1979), 19.

8. Haggai, 21.

9. Nathaniel Branden, *The Psychology of Romantic Love* (Los Angeles: J. P. Tarcher, 1980), 61.

10. McGinnis, 163.

11. Anthony Robbins, *Unlimited Power* (New York: Fawcett Columbine, 1986), 16–19.

12. Ibid., 6.
13. Ibid., 8.
14. Calvin Miller, *If This Be Love* (San Francisco: Harper & Row, 1984), viii.
15. George Barna, *The Power of Vision* (Ventura, Calif.: Regal Books, 1992), 19.
16. Mack Douglas, *How to Make a Habit of Succeeding* (Grand Rapids: Zondervan, 1966), 71.
17. Barna, 138.
18. Warren Bennis, *Why Leaders Can't Lead* (San Francisco: Jossey-Bass Publishers, 1989), 15–16.
19. Ibid., 152.
20. Haggai, 14.

Key 5

1. Obadiah Milton Conover, *Bartlett's Familiar Quotations* (Boston: Little, Brown, and Company, 1968), 562.
2. John C. Maxwell, *Your Attitude: Key to Success* (San Bernardino, Calif.: Here's Life Publishers, Inc., 1984), 66.
3. Peter I. Drucker, *Managing the Non-Profit Organization* (New York: Harper Business, 1990), 71.
4. Philip Greenslade, *Leadership, Greatness, and Servanthood* (Minnesota: Bethany House Publishers, 1984), 72.
5. Drucker, 70.
6. Ted Engstrom, *Seizing the Torch* (Ventura, Calif.: Regal Books, 1988).
7. Burt Nanus, *Visionary Leadership* (San Francisco: Jossey-Bass Publishers, 1992), 83.
8. Maxwell, 25.
9. Ibid.
10. Lee Iacocca with William Novak, *Iacocca: An Autobiography* (New York: Bantam Books, 1984), 141.

11. Viktor E. Frankl, *Man's Search for Meaning* (New York: Simon & Schuster, 1985), 85.

12. Leo Buscaglia, *Politics of Love* (Nightingale-Conant Audio, 1984).

Key 6

1. Anthony Robbins, *Unlimited Power* (New York: Fawcett Columbine, 1986), 200–201.

2. Joe Batten, *Tough-Minded Leadership* (New York: AMACOM, 1989), 45.

3. Ibid., 178–79.

4. James Beall, "How Do You Influence Your People?" *Solving the Ministry's Toughest Problems,* vol. 1 (Altamonte Springs, Fla.: Strang Communications, 1984), 109.

5. Kenneth Blanchard, *The One Minute Manager* (New York: William Merrom and Company, Inc., 1985), 81.

6. Tom Peters, *Thriving on Chaos* (New York: Alfred Knopf, 1987), 410.

7. Blanchard, 46.

Key 7

1. Warren Bennis, *Why Leaders Can't Lead* (San Francisco: Jossey-Bass Publishers, 1989), 41.

2. Ibid., 35.

3. Peter Koestenbaum, *Leadership: The Inner Side of Greatness* (San Francisco: Jossey-Bass Publishers, 1991), 94.

4. Bennis, 22–23.

5. Rollo May, *Love and Will* (New York: Dell Publishing Co., Inc. 1969), 13.

6. Myron C. Madden, *Blessing: Giving the Gift of Power* (Nashville: Broadman Press, 1988), 58.

7. Bennis, 72–73.

8. Ibid., 36.

9. James MacGregor Burns, *Leadership* (New York: Harper & Row, 1979), 61–62.

10. Bennis, 33.

11. Burns, 41.

12. Max DePree, *Leadership Is an Art* (New York: Dell Publishing, 1989), 11.

Key 8

1. Cecil Osborne, *Self-Esteem* (Nashville: Abingdon Press, 1986), 71.

2. David A. Seamands, *Healing of Memories* (Wheaton, Ill.: Victor Books, 1985), 73.

3. Steve Brown, *No More Mr. Nice Guy* (unpublished manuscript), 93.

4. David Augsburger, *Conflict Mediation Across Cultures* (Louisville: Westminster/John Knox Press, 1992), 110.

5. Herb Bisno, *Managing Conflict* (Newburg Park, Calif.: Sage Publishers, 1988), 87.

6. John W. Vale and Robert B. Hughes, *Getting Even* (Grand Rapids: Zondervan Publishers, 1987), 35.

Key 9

1. Warren Bennis and Burt Nanus, *Leaders: The Strategies for Taking Charge* (New York: Harper & Row, 1985), 7.

2. Warren Bennis, *Why Leaders Can't Lead* (San Francisco: Jossey-Bass Publishers, 1989), 18.

3. Ibid., 18.

4. Joe D. Batten, *Tough-Minded Management* (New York: AMACOM, 1963), 19.

5. Ibid., 110.

6. Jim Lundry, *Lead, Follow, or Get Out of the Way* (New York: Berkley Books, 1991), 21.

7. Max DePree, *Leadership Is an Art* (New York: Dell Publishing, 1989), 58.

8. David McKenna, *The Psychology of Jesus* (Waco, Tex.: Word, Inc., 1977), 59.

9. Mack Douglas, *How to Cultivate the Habit of Success* (Grand Rapids: Zondervan Press, 1968), 96.

Key 10

1. Robert D. Dale, *Pastoral Leadership* (Nashville: Abingdon Press, 1986), 158.

2. Eugene B. Habecker, *The Other Side of Leadership* (Wheaton, Ill.: Victor Books, 1987), 103.

3. John Haggai, *Lead On!* (Waco, Tex.: Word Publishers, 1986), 68.

4. Charles Spurgeon, *Treasury of David,* vol. 2, Psalms 27–52 (Grand Rapids: Baker Books, 1984), 451.

5. Robert A. Raines, *Success Is a Moving Target* (Waco, Tex.: Word Books, 1975), 104.

6. Habecker, 109.

Other Able Assistants
for Your Ministry . . .

The Antioch Effect:
8 Characteristics of Highly Effective Churches

Power House:
A Step-by-Step Guide to Building a Church that Prays

The Issachar Factor:
Understanding Trends that Confront Your Church and
Designing a Strategy for Success

Eating the Elephant:
Bite-sized Steps to Achieve Long-term Growth
in Your Church

This bonus section offers help from several specially chosen assistants in the Broadman & Holman group of professional books. The excerpts that follow have been chosen from our other Professional Development Books to give you helpful insights on additional subjects of particular interest to ministers.

The Antioch Effect:

8 Characteristics of Highly Effective Churches
by Ken Hemphill

The "Antioch effect" is what made the church in Acts grow—nurturing the spiritual character of the church. This book helps you focus on developing that character in your church as the foundation for growth, rather than on implementing techniques to make church growth happen.

"Church growth" has become a field of study, a topic of considerable interest and debate, and big business. Growth conferences are sponsored by virtually all evangelical denominations, and at levels from the local church to the national convention. Centers for church growth abound, and seminaries and colleges are getting on the bandwagon. Books, tapes, marketing studies, and models abound. More people are attending more conferences and buying more materials than at any time in the history of the church, and yet little visible results can be detected. Certainly some churches are growing. The mega-church has become the Cinderella story of this decade. New churches are being added to a growing list daily. But is the church growing? Are people being added to the kingdom of God through all this activity? That is another question and one which must be honestly addressed.

In truth, we cannot show substantial church growth. The brutal truth is that church growth is not keeping pace with population increase. Total members in U.S. evangelical churches increased by 28 percent from 1960 to 1990, while population increased by 39 percent. If membership had kept pace with population, we would have 12 million more church members today in the United States.

Our growth in number of churches has not kept pace with the population increase either. The number of churches in the U.S. increased by 7 percent from 1960 to 1990. If the number of churches had grown at the same percentage as population, we would have today an additional 96,000 churches.

Other church growth authors and statisticians have made the same observation. Ken Sidey, in an article in *Christianity Today* acknowledged that our church growth principles don't seem to be working. Statisticians such as Gallup and Barna have consistently and faithfully documented the woeful results of the evangelical community to reach America. Such results have caused some to conclude that the church growth movement is simply not working. While there may be some validity to that accusation, we must ask what would have been the state of the church if there had been no conferences or books to give encouragement and new ideas?

With our focus on methods, models and marketing strategies we're only treating the symptoms of the illness that is robbing the church of its vitality. We're not looking at the true source of the illness. As long as we continue to talk symptoms, we will persist in thinking that we can heal the sickness with another prescription in the form of a new program, method, or model. These too, whether they be traditional or non-traditional, will only provide a surface cure to a problem that is bone deep. If we want to cure the problem that is keeping church growth from taking place, we must go much deeper. It is not so much that our programs, methods, and marketing strategies are out of date. Our primary problem is a spiritual one, not a methodological one.

Church growth is not produced by a program, plan, or marketing strategy. The greatest need of your church is not a clearer understanding of its demographics. The greatest need is a clearer understanding of its God. Church growth is not the result of any program or plan. Church growth is the by-product of a right relationship with the Lord of the church. Church growth is by definition a supernatural activity and thus is accomplished through the church by the Lord Himself. When Jesus founded the church He promised that He Himself would build the church (Matt. 16:18). Paul, in recounting his ministry in Corinth, declared that He planted, Apollos watered, but that God gave the increase (1 Cor. 3:7).

The solution then will not be found in methods, models, or marketing strategies. These are not unimportant issues; they simply are not the primary issue. The church growth movement may have inadvertently produced a subtle sense of carnality in the church. It may have caused some to think that a method or program could produce church growth. Such thinking is both wrong and carnal. "It," whatever cherished program, model, method, or marketing strategy "It" may be, cannot cause your church to grow. Scripture is clear and insistent that God alone can grow His church. The attempt to produce church growth results through a certain method is an attempt to do supernatural work in natural power. This has led to great confusion in many congregations where model after model and method after method have been espoused as the solution to the stagnancy of the church. It has in many cases heaped failure upon failure. So much so that many churches recoil at the very mention of the term "church growth."

Lest you overreact, or think that I am overreacting, I am not arguing against methods, models, marketing strategies, or programs. God is not a God of confusion. He works through human beings and uses strategy and organization. The Scripture is full of illustrations of God working supernaturally through persons with clear strategies. I am simply suggesting that the program is not the first or most crucial issue in relationship to growth. The vast variety of methods and programs being employed sucessfully across our nation will bear powerful testimony to this truth. The critical issue is the supernatural empowering of the church which occurs when the church dwells in right relationship with its Head, Christ.

Thus this book is a foundational book to other books on church growth methodology. It focuses on the character of the church. It addresses the primary question, "What is the character of the church that God has chosen to work through?" We have long recognized and taught that it is the character of an individual that ultimately determines the actions and fruitfulness of that person. I think it is equally true that the character of a church will ultimately determine the ability of that church to grow.

Power House:

A Step-by-Step Guide to Building a Church that Prays
By Glen Martin & Dian Ginter

A well-oiled machine is a joy to behold—intricate parts of all sizes and shapes, close together and yet working smoothly as one. However, the very parts that were designed to work together in perfect, close harmony will tear each other up without proper lubrication. So it is in the church.

Prayer—God's Oil for Relationships

God has provided the wonderful "oil" of prayer, which if properly applied, can help all members work together in spite of the differences. Prayer provides the lubrication so that as a church, made up of different parts, all members can fit together perfectly, working together without friction to perform a job which they could never accomplish on their own.

The same principle is true of the component parts of the church. When heavy duty prayer is applied, the various leadership elements—deacons, trustees, councils, laity, mission groups, etc.—can work in harmony. This means prayer that is enough to saturate the decision-making process, not just a "drop" of prayer at the beginning of a meeting, not just token praying for relationships that do not reach the need, but in-depth praying that not only reaches the needs, but also applies God's oil to the problems, to the points of friction that would otherwise damage or destroy things of value. This really means the whole machine needs oil on an ongoing basis.

Looking further at this illustration, in the world of machinery different kinds of oils—various grades and different weights—are used for a specific need. To apply too light an oil when a heavy duty one is needed can lead to trouble. Too heavy an oil where a light one is called for may gum up the works or be overkill.

The same concept applies to prayer. There are different kinds of prayer for different kinds of situations. God has shown us how to pray for certain results, confess when appropriate, intercede for others, and do spiritual warfare in cific situations. Each fills a need and, when used appropriately, can be the very oil to make our lives and our churches run their best.

A powerful house of prayer is a church that knows the value of the oil of prayer. It is using prayer to maximize all of its ministries and to maintain a smooth running operation. Prayer is acting as a shield against any of the enemy's attacks on all ministries and relationships. This shield of prayer concept will be developed more in chapter 4.

Prayer Ministry vs. House of Prayer

At this point a distinction should be drawn between having a prayer ministry and desiring to be a house of prayer. A prayer ministry involves a portion of the congregation in ministry, as with a youth ministry. A limited number will be involved—usually, those with a greater burden for prayer. Such a ministry may take the form of missionary prayer circles; times of prayer open to the whole church such as a prayer meeting; or men's/women's/youth's prayer meeting; a prayer room; an intercessory team; prayer ministry before/during/after the church service; or a prayer chain. In such cases, prayer will be seen as something done by some but not all of the membership. It will be just another, although important, ministy, as is evangelism or choir.

Some churches have tried to solve this problem by creating a prayer room in their facility, thinking this is the equivalent of becoming a house of prayer. The prayer room can be a very helpful component of the prayer life of a church but should not be the main focus. It is only a part of the overall prayer picture.

All prayer ministries are important, for they lay the foundation for becoming a house of prayer since there is already an acknowledgment of the strategic importance of prayer in the church. God will help you build on your current ministry and help you go to the next level of prayer, until you truly become a powerful house of prayer.

The Issachar Factor

Understanding Trends that Confront Your Church and Designing a Strategy for Success
by Glen Martin & Gary McIntosh

Martin and McIntosh help you learn how to meet the needs of a modern congregation in a biblical way by transforming troubling trends into ministry opportunities. The title is taken from 1 Chronicles: "The sons of Issachar . . . understood the times and knew what Israel should do."

During the last half century, we have lived in a virtual explosion of information. More information has been produced in the last thirty years than in the previous five thousand. Today, information doubles every five years. By the year 2000 it will be doubling every four years! For example, note the following signs of the information explosion experienced since the 1940s.

• *Computers:* Between 1946 and 1960 the number of computers grew from one to ten thousand, and from 1960 to 1980 to ten million. By the year 2000 there will be over eighty million computers in the United States alone. The number of components that can be programmed into a computer chip is doubling every eighteen months.

• *Publications:* Approximately ninety-six hundred different periodicals are published in the United States each year, and about one thousand books are published internationally every day. Printed information doubles every eight years. A weekday edition of the *New York Times* contains more information than the average person was likely to come across in a lifetime in seventeenth-century England.

• *Libraries:* The world's great libraries are doubling in size every fourteen years. In the early 1300s, the Sorbonne Library in Paris contained only 1,338 books and yet was thought to be the largest library in Europe. Today several libraries in the world have an inventory of well over eight million books each.

• *Periodicals:* The Magazine Publishers Association notes that 265 more magazines were published in 1988 than in

1989, which works out to about one a day if magazine creators take weekends off. Newsstands offer a choice of twenty-five hundred different magazines.

• *Reference works:* The Pacific Bell Yellow pages are used about 3.5 million times a day. There are 33 million copies of 108 different directories with 41 billion pages of information. The new second edition of the *Random House Dictionary* of the English Language contains more than 315,000 words, has 2,500 pages, weighs 13.5 pounds, and has 50,000 new entries.

All of this information is good. Right? Wrong! Today we must deal with new challenges like overload amnesia, which occurs when an individual's brain shuts down to protect itself. Did you ever forget simple information like a friend's name when trying to introduce them to another person? That's overload amnesia. Or have you ever crammed for an exam only to forget what it was about less than one hour later? That's "Chinese-dinner memory dysfunction"—an undue emphasis on short-term memory. Or have you ever read about an upcoming event in a church program only to forget about it later? That's a result of "informational cacophony"—too much exposure to information so that you end up reading or hearing something but not remembering it. Finally, consider VCRitis—buying a high-technology product, getting it home, and then not being able to program it.

Exposure to this proliferation of information has created a generation of people with different needs, needs which require new models of ministry. The problem is that many churches continue to use models of ministry which do not address the different needs people have today. Examine the following effects of the information age. Ministry must change to meet people's needs today.

• People have less free time and are more difficult to recruit.
• People oppose change, resist making friends, and are lonely.
• People are bombarded by so much information that they find it difficult to listen to more information.
• People cannot see the big picture, tie the ends together, or see how the pieces relate.

- People hear more than they understand, forget what they already know, and resist learning more.
- People don't know how to use what they learn, make mistakes when they try, and fell guilty about it.
- People know information is out there, have difficulty getting it, and make mistakes without it.

Changing Models

Even though we minister in the information age, churches continue to reflect their agricultural and industrial age roots. This leads to stress as programs that worked in the past are not as effective today. Consider these two examples.

Worship services at 11:00 A.M. are a throwback to the agricultural age when churches had to give farmers time to complete the morning chores, hitch the horse to the wagon, and drive into town. The time most farmers completed this routine, 11:00 A.M., was the logical choice for morning church services to begin. Today, however, many churches find earlier hours for worship services often attract more people.

The evening service is a throwback to the industrial age when electric lights were first developed. Initially not every home or business establishment was able to have lights installed. Some enterprising church leaders found that by installing electric lights they could attract crowds to evening evangelistic church services. Today many churches find that smaller groups meeting in homes attract more people than evening services.

Let's face it: Most church models of ministry were developed in an entirely different age. The models of ministry developed in the agricultural and industrial ages are colliding head-on with the information age. That's what this book is all about. Our nation has changed; people have changed; and we must develop new models of ministry relevant for today's society if we are to fulfill Christ's commission to "make disciples."

While it is not possible to cover every aspect of ministry, throughout this book you'll find not only insight as to what changes have taken place, but also practical ideas you can use immediately to be more effective in your own ministry.

To get the best value from this book first overview the entire contents. You will find that each chapter focuses on areas of ministry commonly found in churches. If you are involved in a ministry specifically addressed by one chapter, read that chapter first and begin to use some of the practical suggestions immediately. Then go back through the other chapters, carefully noting insights and ideas applicable to other ministries in your church.

People of Issachar

In the Old Testament there's an interesting story in 1 Chronicles 12. David had been running from Saul, and while he was hiding, God sent some men to him who are described as mighty men of valor. The first group of men were skilled with the bow, with the arrow, and with the sling. These men would stand behind the lines and shoot arrows and fling stones over the front lines to inflict wounds on the enemy. Other men were skilled in the use of the shield and the sword, moved swiftly, and had a tenacious spirit. They would fight one on one with the enemy at the front lines. A third category of men understood the times and knew what Israel should do. They were the strategists who developed the master plan for the battle. We today need to be like men of Issachar. We need to be people who understand our times, know what we should do, and have the courage to do it.

We trust that *The Issachar Factor* will help you understand the times in which you are called to minister and know what to do to increase your church's effectiveness.

Eating the Elephant

Bite-sized Steps to Achieve Long-term Growth in Your Church
by Thom S. Rainer

Eating the Elephant shows why, in many cases, "contemporary" church growth plans can do more harm than good. It also explains how the long road to lasting growth is best traveled in tiny steps—through creating sensitive change at a comfortable pace.

Most pastors realize that some type of change must take place in their churches in order to reach effectively a growing unchurched population. Many pastors face two major obstacles: lack of know-how and the inability to apply known principles of change.

Generally, innovations can be implemented with relative ease in three cases: (1) a newly-planted church; (2) a church that has experienced rapid growth due to relocation; or (3) a church that still has its founding pastor. Churches in these three categories account for less than 10 percent of all Christian churches in America. What do the remaining 90-percent-plus churches do? Can they be effective? Can they make a difference in their communities? Can they reach the unchurched? Can they implement change without destroying their fellowship?

Such is the tension that exists in many of the so-called traditional churches. How can the church be relevant to both the growing unchurched population and to the members for whom church relevance is grounded in old hymns and long-standing methodologies? The good news is that the traditional church can grow. Through my contact with hundreds of such churches in America, I have discovered that many pastors are leading traditional churches to growth. I will share with you their principles and struggles. And I will share with you my own successes and failures of leading traditional churches to growth.

Many of my church members know that I love a good, clean joke. One of them shared with me a series of elephant jokes.

One of the jokes asked the question: "How do you eat an elephant?" The answer: "One bite at a time." Later I would realize that the joke describes well the task before any leader in a traditional church. The process of leading a traditional church to growth is analogous to "eating an elephant." It is a long-term deliberate process that must be implemented "one bite at a time."

If the task before us is eating an elephant, then we must avoid two extremes. The first extreme is to ignore the task at hand. I remember when my son Sam had a monumental science project to complete. He was overwhelmed by the enormity of the task. Working together, we established a list of items to be completed and the date by which each item had to be finished. Instead of being a burden, the project became a joy because he could see his daily progress. Much to his amazement and delight, Sam finished the assignment several days before the deadline.

If we acknowledge that our churches are far from effective, the challenge to change may seem overwhelming. You are in the same situation as most pastors in America. But with God's anointing, you can lead toward change and growth one step at a time.

On the other hand, we must avoid the other extreme of eating the elephant in just a few bites. Massive and sudden change (I realize "massive" is a relative term but, for many church members, their "massive" is the pastor's "slight.") can divide and demoralize a traditional church. Remember, church members who hold tenaciously to the old paradigms are not "wrong" while you are "right." They are children of God loved no less by the Father than those who prefer a different style.